CHINESE EDUCATION AND SOCIETY
A BIBLIOGRAPHIC GUIDE

THE CULTURAL REVOLUTION
AND ITS AFTERMATH

Stewart E. Fraser and
Kuang-liang Hsu

LONDON AND NEW YORK

First published 1972 by International Arts and Sciences Press, Inc.

Reissued 2018 by Routledge
2 Park Square, Milton Park, Abingdon, Oxon OX14 4RN
711 Third Avenue, New York, NY 10017, USA

Routledge is an imprint of the Taylor & Francis Group, an informa business

Copyright © 1972 by Taylor & Francis

No part of this book may be reprinted or reproduced or utilised in any form or by any electronic, mechanical, or other means, now known or hereafter invented, including photocopying and recording, or in any information storage or retrieval system, without permission in writing from the publishers.

Notices
No responsibility is assumed by the publisher for any injury and/or damage to persons or property as a matter of products liability, negligence or otherwise, or from any use of operation of any methods, products, instructions or ideas contained in the material herein.

Practitioners and researchers must always rely on their own experience and knowledge in evaluating and using any information, methods, compounds, or experiments described herein. In using such information or methods they should be mindful of their own safety and the safety of others, including parties for whom they have a professional responsibility.

Product or corporate names may be trademarks or registered trademarks, and are used only for identification and explanation without intent to infringe.

Publisher's Note
The publisher has gone to great lengths to ensure the quality of this reprint but points out that some imperfections in the original copies may be apparent.

Disclaimer
The publisher has made every effort to trace copyright holders and welcomes correspondence from those they have been unable to contact.

A Library of Congress record exists under LC control number: 72077206

ISBN 13: 978-0-87332-005-4 (hbk)
ISBN 13: 978-1-138-89741-0 (pbk)
ISBN 13: 978-1-315-17889-9 (ebk)

To Francis Neel Cheney

Contents

Introduction: Notes on Bibliographic Sources, Selected
Research Centers, and Publications   1

Standard Abbreviations   14

I.   Bibliography, Reference, and Documentation   15

II.   General Survey and Background   33

III.   Great Proletarian Cultural Revolution   45

IV.   General Survey of Education   83

V.   Primary (Elementary) Education   91

VI.   Secondary (Middle) Education   97

VII.   Teaching and Teacher Education   105

VIII.   Higher Education   113

IX.   Agricultural and Rural Education   137

X.   Youth and Student Affairs   149

XI.   International Relations in Education   155

XII.   Ideology and Education   161

XIII.   Educational Development and the Great
Proletarian Cultural Revolution (1966-1968)   177

XIV.   Mao Tse-tung's Educational Thought   199

Acknowledgements

Acknowledgement is gratefully made of the assistance provided by staff members of the Peabody International Center for their kind and generous help in the compilation and preparation of this bibliography. In particular, appreciation is due Lucille Hood, Gayla Tinnell, Marie Williams, John N. Hawkins, and Shiao Chung Hu.

Appreciation should be expressed to the University of London Institute of Education Libraries, the publisher of Education Libraries Bulletin, and to its Director, D. J. Foskett, and editor, Michael J. Humby, for facilitating the publication of this bibliography.

We are indebted to Peter J. Seybolt, of the University of Vermont, for reading the manuscript and offering a variety of helpful suggestions.

Introduction:

NOTES ON BIBLIOGRAPHIC SOURCES, SELECTED RESEARCH
CENTERS, AND PUBLICATIONS

The materials included in this bibliography are derived from
English- and Chinese-language sources (which predominate),
as well as from Japanese, French, German, and Italian
publications. The majority of references are available in
English-language publications or translations. Those sources
which are solely in the Chinese language are listed in romanized form with a concurrent English title. References are
made to a variety of bibliographies, biographical dictionaries,
yearbooks, dictionaries of terminology, and similar standard
works. These have been published during or after the Cultural
Revolution and do not include pre-1966 publications.

For the reader's convenience this bibliography is divided
into fourteen sections, I through XIV, under functional headings
such as Elementary (Primary) Education, Secondary (Middle)
Education, Higher Education, etc. Within each major section,
references are arranged alphabetically by authors, though, in
the case (especially for primary sources) where authorship
is not otherwise identified, materials are entered under publication source. Cross references are provided for almost half
of the items which could be classified under more than one
heading. Accordingly, for the complete annotation the reader
should consult the appropriate section as indicated at the end
of each cross reference, i.e., [II] stands for section II of the
bibliography.

Major English-language sources on education noted in this
bibliography are available from the following four geographical research areas (1): Hong Kong, B.C.C.; Taiwan; the United
States; and the People's Republic of China.

1

2

From Hong Kong (B.C.C.)

In the British Crown Colony of Hong Kong, an extensive range of material on Chinese Communist education has been compiled in both Chinese- and English-language editions. These compilations are based on a variety of Chinese Communist newspapers and periodicals. Two major organizations are engaged in compiling and translating these materials: the American Consulate General in Hong Kong and the Union Research Institute (URI).

In 1950, a press and translation unit was established in the United States Consulate General in Hong Kong to develop a regular flow of materials on China (PRC). The principal English-language translation series of the Consulate are compiled as follows:

1. Current Background, published since June 1950 on an ad hoc basis, usually weekly. Each issue generally focuses on a single aspect of Chinese Communism and is a compilation from various newspaper and periodical articles. Major economic and political conferences are thoroughly documented in the translation, and a chronology of principal developments is presented periodically.

2. Survey of China Mainland Press, published since November 1950. It is the major serial of the translation services issued by the Consulate and covers a carefully selected range of activities in China (PRC). The Survey regularly carries the main governmental press releases of the New China News Agency and of the influential Jen-min jih-pao [People's Daily].

3. Extracts from China Mainland Magazines, published since August 1955 on an ad hoc basis, sometimes weekly. Translations are made in full of periodical articles from various journals such as Jen-min chiao-yü [People's Education], Hsüeh-hsi [Study], and Ch'iao-wu pao [Overseas Chinese Affairs Journal]. In 1962, Extracts . . . became Selections from China Mainland Magazines.

4. Review of the Hong Kong Chinese Press, published from 1950 to 1961. It was issued daily and contained résumés of

both the pro-Nationalist and pro-Communist press.

Since 1956, Current Background, Survey of China Mainland Press, and Extracts from China Mainland Magazines have been regularly indexed. The cumulative issues of Current Background and Survey of China Mainland Press from 1950 to 1955 have recently been indexed as well.

5. Current Scene, Developments in Mainland China (USIS) consists of a monthly series of well-documented monographs on various aspects of Chinese political, economic, and educational developments; it began appearing in 1962.

6. China Reporting Service (USIS) provided features and graphics on China; it merged with Current Scene on July 24, 1970.

Since February 1971, the first three publications (items 1-3) have been available from Clearinghouse, U.S. Department of Commerce, Springfield, Virginia, U.S.A., on a subscription basis.

The Union Research Institute (URI) in Hong Kong also engages in translating and compiling English-language studies on various aspects of Chinese Communism. The URI was first established in Nanking in 1948 and reestablished in Hong Kong in January 1951 as a division of the Union Press. The Institute has accumulated a vast collection of materials concerning China (PRC), mostly publications by the Chinese Communists. The materials, covering the entire period since the establishment of the Communist government, have been minutely classified, microfilmed, and indexed.

URI regularly acquires some 95 Chinese newspapers and approximately 230 periodicals from the People's Republic of China and the Republic of China and other parts of Asia. Over 4 million classified and indexed clippings are now in its files. These are divided into six basic sections: Political and Social Affairs, Finance and Economics, Education and Culture (including Science and Technology), Military Affairs, Overseas Chinese, and International Communism.

Its library contains approximately 30,000 books and pamphlets; about 80 percent are from China (PRC) and are not

4

readily obtainable in Hong Kong or elsewhere. They include a unique collection of nearly 400 textbooks published for use in primary and high schools.

The Institute has produced a valuable English-language publication series entitled Communist China Problem Research Series, which includes several titles on education. In addition, the Institute provides twice weekly a translation service of materials from China mainland regional newspapers which are not easily available. (See Union Research Service Series.) The Institute prepares useful monographs on Chinese education and makes available to researchers its index of acquisitions and translations.

A weekly newsletter, the China News Analysis, published in Hong Kong since August 1953, has become one of the most valuable sources of critical analytical information on China. Many of the editions are devoted to educational and related matters.

Other organizations in Hong Kong engaged in research and publishing on contemporary China are the Continental Research Institute, the Asia Research Center, Contemporary China Research Institute, China Problems Research Center, Center of Contemporary Chinese Studies, and the China Research Associates.

The Institute for Asian Studies at the University of Hong Kong and the East Asian Institute of the Chinese University of Hong Kong are both newly established, and their research programs are currently in the process of development.

The Universities Service Centre in Hong Kong provides extensive research facilities but has not embarked on a detailed research or publication program.

Peking Informers (bimonthly), China Problems Research Monthly, Far Eastern Economic Review, Eastern Horizon, Takung pao Weekly Supplement, Ming-pao yüeh-k'an [Ming Pao Monthly], Ming-pao chou-k'an [Ming Pao Weekly], and Chungkuo p'ing-lun [China Review Weekly] also publish, on an ad hoc basis, a variety of short articles on Chinese education.

From Taiwan

Several research groups in Taiwan, principally in Taipei, are actively engaged in studying Chinese Communist problems for reasons of both academic research and intelligence analysis. The Institute of International Relations was established in 1961 under a charter from the Ministry of Education, Republic of China. The Institute acquires, compiles, publishes, and disseminates materials on Communist China and other related subjects. It has four research sections: (1) International Affairs Research Group, (2) Soviet Bloc Affairs Research Group, (3) Chinese Communist Affairs Research Group, and (4) Economic Affairs Research Group. Each group carries out collective research projects, as well as individual research studies. Research findings on Communist China are published variously in book form and in periodicals both in Chinese and in English. The English-language journal Issues & Studies has been published monthly since October 1964. Beginning in Volume V, No. 10, July 1969, the journal contains articles and notes on current affairs, documents, and personalities, as well as book reviews and a chronicle of events pertaining to the Chinese mainland. Chinese-language journals published by the Institute include Fei-ch'ing yüeh-pao [Chinese Communist Affairs Monthly] and Wen-t'i yü yen-chiu [Issues & Studies] (in Chinese — the contents are not identical with the English-language journal Issues & Studies).

In addition to the above-mentioned activities, the Institute also maintains a collection of materials on Chinese Communism of approximately 50,000 books and monographs, 100,000 classified newspaper clippings, and a Union Catalog. (2)

The Institute of Mainland China Affairs (Taipei), established in 1962, is another organization that carries out research and publishes materials on Communist China (post-1949). Its publications are mainly in the Chinese language. Its series Ta-lu wen-t'i chuan-t'i yen-chiu [Studies of Special Topics on Mainland China Affairs] and its periodical Chung-kung tung-tai fen-hsi [An Analysis of Chinese Communist Current Affairs],

6

published since September 1965, were merged in March 1971 to form a new periodical under the title Chung-kuo ta-lu yen-chiu [Mainland China Studies]; it is published semimonthly.

The Institute for the Study of Chinese Communist Problems (Taipei) has published monthly since January 1967 a periodical entitled Fei-ch'ing yen-chiu (3) [Studies on Chinese Communism] and Fei-ch'ing nien-pao (4) [Yearbook on Chinese Communism]. Both are Chinese-language publications.

From the United States

The advancement of library collection facilities and information retrieval techniques in the United States (5) has encouraged the growth of a number of compilations and publications on contemporary Chinese society and education. Probably the most significant publication on education to date, and the only one of its kind in the English language, is the quarterly publication Chinese Education, published since 1968 by International Arts and Sciences Press in White Plains, New York. This is a specialist journal devoted to translations on educational topics concerning modern China.

The Joint Publications Research Service (JPRS), a component of the Clearinghouse for Federal Scientific and Technical Information of the Department of Commerce, was established in March 1957 to provide government agencies with translations of unclassified foreign documents of importance from over 125 countries. Over 250,000 pages of translations per year are available in microfilm, microfiche, microprint, or Xerox Copyflo format. The translations are divided into Social Science (SS) and Scientific-Technical (ST) sections. About 40 percent of the translations are in the first section and 60 percent in the latter section. Over 775 scientific-technical journals form the basis for sources of the translated documents in the ST section, of which 71 are from the People's Republic of China.

The subject range on China covers accounting system, administration, agriculture, biography, botany, cities, climate, communes, Communist Party, constitution, conservation, economic geography, economics, education, ethnography, foreign relations, geography, geology, housing, industry, law, natural resources, politics, provinces, science, and transportation. (6) The types of materials translated include abstracts, atlases, bibliographies, digests, directories, gazetteers, guides, handbooks, lectures, manuals, reports, surveys, etc.

Cheng-fa yen-chiu [Political and Legal Research], Chiao-yü pan-yüeh-k'an [Education Semimonthly], Ching-chi yen-chiu [Economics Research], Hsin-hua pan-yüeh-k'an [New China Semimonthly], Hung-ch'i [Red Flag], and Jen-min chiao-yü [People's Education] are just a few of the journal titles utilized for source material in the Social Science section.

In addition to the translations from the People's Republic of China, JPRS also translates materials concerning that nation (PRC) from other countries, especially from the USSR.

Furthermore, JPRS issues the Communist China Digest, which is a serial publication of summaries or extracts from selected reports concerning major aspects of Chinese life and society. For example, "Great Proletarian Cultural Revolution" formed the major part of No. 186 of Communist China Digest (JPRS 41450).

The Foreign Broadcasting Information Service (FBIS), Washington, D.C., provides another important source of translated materials. Like the JPRS, it also publishes special issues on certain topics, including education and cultural affairs. (7)

The U.S. Office of Education is another official governmental organization which publishes occasional papers, research, and monographs on special topics in the field of Asian Communist education by distinguished experts. USOE publications are listed in the Monthly Catalog of United States Government Publications.

A number of American universities have established centers for Chinese studies, among them, for example, the University of California (Berkeley), Columbia, Harvard, the University of Washington, Cornell, the University of Michigan. Some of these centers publish monograph series, e.g., the University

8

of California Center for Chinese Studies began publishing "China Research Monographs" in 1967, and "Studies in Chinese Communist Terminology" in 1956. The University of Michigan Center for Chinese Studies publishes "Michigan Papers in Chinese Studies."

The Hoover Institution on War, Revolution, and Peace, founded in 1919 at Stanford University, is a research center and library devoted to twentieth century political, social, and economic problems, with special emphasis on communism, revolutionary movements, peace movements, World Wars I and II, and international relations.

The Institution houses under one roof research scholars, area specialists (curators) in charge of acquisitions and collecting activities, a specialized library, and archives. It publishes over 30 volumes every year, including bibliographies and checklists of its library holdings (8) and monographs by research scholars at the Institution and by other scholars on subjects of contemporary interest.

Hoover began collecting materials on Chinese Communism in 1945 and since then has continued to stress its interest in modern China, thus enabling the Institution to maintain its position as the holder of one of the best collections on this area. In 1967 the Institution published a most comprehensive research guide on contemporary China, entitled Contemporary China: A Research Guide, compiled by Peter Berton and Eugene Wu. (The termination date for the publications included in this Guide is 1963.)

Another source for current research on China can be found in Ph.D. dissertations completed in American universities. From 1949 to 1971, some 120 Ph.D. dissertations on China have been accepted by American universities. These dissertations are available on microfilm or xerography facsimiles from University Microfilms, Ann Arbor, Michigan.

The British Embassy in Washington, D.C., issues China Topics and China Record in mimeographed form.

Sinologists concerned with education and comparative educators in the United States publish their studies in a variety

of social science and educational journals. Such ad hoc
contributors on Chinese Communist education include:
Robert D. Barendsen (Office of Education), Theodore Hsi-en
Chen (Southern California), Chu-yuan Cheng (Michigan), J.
Chester Cheng (San Francisco State), Stewart E. Fraser (Pea-
body), John N. Hawkins (Peabody), C. T. Hu (Columbia), Leo
A. Orleans (Library of Congress), Allen B. Linden (New Hamp-
shire), Peter J. Seybolt (Vermont), and Cho-yee To (Michigan).

The following is a partial list of various American journals
containing articles on education or of relevance to this field.

1. Asian Survey (Berkeley)
2. Bulletin of the Atomic Scientists (Chicago) (9)
3. China Science Notes (National Academy of Sciences et al.,
   Washington, D.C.)
4. Chinese Education (White Plains, New York), contains
   translation of articles from Chinese education journals.
5. Chinese Sociology and Anthropology (White Plains, New
   York), a journal of translations.
6. Communist Affairs (Los Angeles)
7. Comparative Education Review (Wisconsin) (10)
8. Current History (Philadelphia), September issues are
   devoted to the study of Communist China.
9. Foreign Broadcasting Information Service (FBIS)
   Washington, D.C., provides translated materials and
   publishes special issues on selected topics.
10. The Journal of Asian Studies (Ann Arbor), provides a
    comprehensive annual bibliography on Asian studies, in
    addition to its regular issues. (11)
11. Pacific Affairs (Honolulu and Vancouver)
12. Problems of Communism (Washington, D.C.) (12)
13. School and Society (New York) (13)

From the People's Republic of China

Since the translated materials in the English-language compilations noted above do not cover comprehensively all the
publications appearing in China, magazines and newspapers

10

released directly from Peking constitute another important source of primary material.(14) While a number of Chinese-language educational journals are available in major libraries in the United States (Library of Congress, for example), there are in addition a variety of English-language publications issued by the Foreign Languages Press, Peking. (15) The following publications in both Chinese and English are especially useful for the study of Chinese education, and some have provided material included in this bibliography. (16)

1. Afro-Asian Journalist
2. The Call
3. Chiao-hsüeh yü yen-chiu [Teaching and Research]
4. China Pictorial (Monthly)
5. China Reconstructs (Monthly)
6. China's Medicine (Bimonthly) (Including materials on medical education)
7. Chinese Literature (Monthly)
8. Chung-kuo ch'ing-nien [Chinese Youth] (Ceased publication in August 1966)
9. Chung-kuo ch'ing-nien pao [China Youth News] (Ceased publication in September 1966)
10. Chung-kuo hsin-wen [China News Service, Canton] (Daily)
11. Chung-kuo yü-wen [Chinese Language]
12. Evergreen (Ceased publication in 1967)
13. Hsiao-hsüeh chiao-shih [Primary Schoolteacher]
14. Hsin chien-she [New Construction]
15. Hsinhua News Agency Release
16. Hsinhua Weekly Issue
17. Hsüeh-hsi [Study]
18. Hung-ch'i [Red Flag] (Monthly)
19. Jen-min chiao-yü [People's Education]
20. Jen-min hua-pao [China Pictorial]
21. Jen-min jih-pao [People's Daily]
22. Jen-min wen-hsüeh [People's Literature]
23. Kuang-ming jih-pao [Kuang-ming Daily]
24. Kung-jen jih-pao [Worker's Daily] (Ceased publication in January 1967)

25. Peking Review (Weekly)
26. Ta kung pao [Takung Daily, Peking] (Ceased publication in October 1966)
27. Wen-hsüeh p'ing-lun [Literary Review]
28. Wen-tzu kai-ke [Language Reform]

Notes

1) These notes are intended to cover principally the aforementioned areas only and accordingly do not include information as to sources, publications, and research centers to be found in other areas such as Western Europe or Australasia, etc.

2) Warren Kuo, "Research on Chinese Communist Affairs in the Republic of China," Issues & Studies, 7 (January 1971), 15-20.

3) This title should not be confused with another periodical under the same title, Fei-ch'ing yen-chiu [Study of Chinese Communist Affairs], which has been published irregularly since March 1958 by the Bureau of Intelligence, Ministry of National Defense, Republic of China. (This publication is not for sale or public distribution.)

4) Beginning with 1969, the Chinese title has been changed to Chung-kung nien-pao. [N.B. Literally Fei-ch'ing nien-pao, meaning "Bandit Affairs Yearbook," changed to Chung-kung nien-pao or "Chinese Communist Yearbook."]

5) See Paul Wong, "Storage and Retrieval of Data on Communist China," Asian Survey, 8 (May 1968), 378-383.

6) These subjects follow the classification used in the Subject Index of Transdex: Guide to U.S. Government JPRS Translations of Iron-Curtain Documents (Monthly, Collier-Macmillan International, New York).

7) For example, a special compilation of early documents on the GPCR is contained in four supplements under the subtitle: Material on Cultural Revolution, Vol. I, FB101/67/07S, 24 May 1967, 60 pp.; Vol. II, FB108/67/10S, 5 June 1967, 72 pp.; Vol. III, FB113/67/11S, 12 June 1967, 90 pp.; and Vol. IV, FB119/67/13S, 20 June 1967, 74 pp.

8) The complete catalog of the Institution's library was

12

published in 1970 by G. K. Hall & Co., Boston, Mass., entitled: The Library Catalogs of the Hoover Institution on War, Revolution, and Peace, Stanford University. 10 x 14: Catalog of the Western Language Collection, est. 1,101,000 cards, 63 volumes. Catalogs of the Western Language Serials and Newspaper Collections, est. 46,000 cards, 3 volumes. Catalog of the Chinese Collection, est. 201,000 cards, 13 volumes. Catalog of the Japanese Collection, est. 125,000 cards, 7 volumes. Catalog of the Arabic Collection, est. 18,900 cards, 1 volume. Catalogs of the Turkish and Persian Collections, est. 14,000 cards, 1 volume.

9) The entire issue of Vol. 25, No. 2, February 1969, is devoted to a symposium on "China After the Cultural Revolution."

10) The entire issue of Vol. 13, No. 1, February 1969, is devoted to a "Symposium on Aspects of Chinese Education."

11) Its annual bibliographies before the end of 1965 have been accumulated and published by G. K. Hall & Co., Boston, Mass., in 1970, in a four-volume set entitled: Cumulative Bibliography of Asian Studies, 1941-1965.

12) For example, five series of articles on the GPCR under the heading "The New Revolution" were published in this journal in Vol. 15, No. 6, November-December 1966; Vol. 16, No. 2, March-April 1967; Vol. 16, No. 3, May-June 1967; and Vol. 17, No. 2, March-April 1968.

13) Important Chinese educational documents are published on an ad hoc basis in this journal. For research and resources for the study of contemporary China outside the United States, see Eugene W. Wu, "Studies of Contemporary China Outside the United States," Harvard Library Bulletin (April 18, 1970), 141-154.

14) There were 648 periodicals available on subscription through the post offices in China in 1966, 132 in 1967, only 58 in 1968. See John T. Ma, "Collecting Research Materials on Post-1949 Mainland China," Issues & Studies, 7 (January 1971), 35.

15) For example, the Foreign Languages Press, Peking, published from 1966 to 1967 a collection of documents and editorials from major newspapers concerning the GPCR entitled The Great Socialist Cultural Revolution.

16) Because of the ideological conflicts, purges of editors, political struggle, or other reasons, some of these publications have been suspended since the GPCR, viz., Chung-kuo ch'ing-nien, Evergreen. However, the inclusion of these titles is for background reference for the period prior to the GPCR. Recent information suggests that some defunct publications will soon be revived and/or new periodicals published.

Standard abbreviations

CB	Current Background
CCP	Chinese Communist Party
CCPCC	Chinese Communist Party Central Committee
CFCP	Chieh-fang-chün pao
CNA	China News Analysis (Hong Kong)
CPPCC	Chinese People's Political Consultative Conference
FBIS	Foreign Broadcast Information Service
GPCR	Great Proletarian Cultural Revolution
IIR	Institute of International Relations (Taipei)
JMJP	Jen-min jih-pao [People's Daily]
JPRS	Joint Publication Research Service
KMJP	Kuang-ming jih-pao [Kuangming Daily]
NCNA	New China News Agency
PRC	People's Republic of China
SCMM	Selections from China Mainland Magazines
SCMP	Survey of China Mainland Press
TMTT	Thought of Mao Tse-tung
URI	Union Research Institute (Hong Kong)
URS	Union Research Service (Hong Kong)
USIS	United States Information Service

I. Bibliography, reference, and documentation

BERTON, Peter, and Eugene Wu. Contemporary China: A Research Guide. Stanford, Calif.: Hoover Institution on War, Revolution, and Peace, 1967. 695 pp.

Directed principally at the social sciences and humanities, and dealing almost entirely with post-1949 China (PRC) and post-1945 Taiwan, this volume covers biographical and reference works; selected documentary materials on law, politics, government, foreign relations, economics, education, and culture; and selected serial publications. Sources are from China (PRC), Taiwan, Hong Kong, Japan, the United States, Great Britain, the USSR, and elsewhere.

CCP Documents of the Great Proletarian Cultural Revolution, 1966-1967. Hong Kong: Union Research Institute, 1968. 692 pp.

A collection of 132 documents, including 122 issued by CCP central authorities and 10 by the Peking municipal authorities in 1966 and 1967 concerning the Great Proletarian Cultural Revolution. Ten of the documents were published officially; and 25 of the documents are published in this book in English for the first time. Documents are published in bilingual form: Chinese texts and English translations. The official English edition of the documents is used whenever available. Editorials and articles are not included in this collection.

The Case of P'eng Teh-huai, 1959-1968. Hong Kong: Union Research Institute, 1968. 515 pp.

16

A compilation of 41 documents on the case of P'eng Te-huai including his "letter of opinion," dated July 14, 1959, and his "testimony," dated January 5, 1967, when he was in custody of the Red Guards. Appendices include "Revolt of the Generals" by Lois Dougan Tretiak, a 46-page chronology of P'eng's career, and Chinese texts of 23 documents. Introduction by Kung Chu, former comrade-in-arms of P'eng Te-huai.

CHENG, Peter. A Chronology of the People's Republic of China: From October 1, 1949. Totowa, New Jersey: Rowman and Littlefield, 1972. 347 pp.

A daily record of events concerning the People's Republic of China from October 1, 1949, to December 20, 1969. The record, while extensive, is incomplete, some educational and cultural events being omitted. The index is limited to geographical/national and a few broad subject categories.

China Topics. "China's Education Problems." YB 427 (May 23, 1967).

Documentation on the problems of reopening of schools in China. Information is taken mainly from press and radio sources. Followed by six appendices of documents on educational reform: "Draft Recommendations on Educational Reform"; "Directive on Cultural Revolution in Middle Schools"; "Directive on Cultural Revolution in Universities, Colleges and Institutes"; "Ch'en Yi on Educational Reform"; "Ch'en Po-ta and Chi Pen-yu on Educational Reform"; and "Protests Against Special Boarding Schools for Cadres' Children."

Chinese Communist Who's Who. Vol. I. Taipei: Institute of International Relations, 1970. 454 pp.

Includes 1,062 names listed alphabetically from Ai to Li. The original Chinese-language version of the volume was

17

first published in August 1967. This English-language version is a revised and enlarged edition of the original edition. It has, for example, included new CCP Central Committee members elected at the Ninth CCP National Congress of April 1969. Mistakes made in the earlier edition are corrected, and information needing further confirmation has been omitted.

Chung-kung shu-yu hui-chieh [A Glossary of Chinese Communist Terminology]. Taipei: China Publishing Co., 1971. 455 pp.

Contains 1,232 terms used from the establishment of the Chinese Communist Party to its post-Ninth CCP National Congress (i.e., late 1970) development. The terms in the book cover Party, military, political, economic, cultural, and educational affairs. They are arranged by number of strokes of Chinese characters rather than by functional categories. Original materials are frequently quoted in the definitions.

Collected Documents of the First Sino-American Conference on Mainland China. Taipei: Institute of International Relations, 1971. 951 pp.

Contains 6 reports and 33 papers presented to the First Sino-American Conference on Mainland China sponsored by the Institute of International Relations, Republic of China, from December 13 through 19, 1970. The papers are grouped under 5 categories: (I) history and personnel affairs, (II) ideology and education, (III) politics, (IV) the economy, and (V) military affairs. Papers in section II are "An Analysis of the Thought of Mao Tse-tung," by Jen Cho-hsuan; "Student Exchange in Communist China," by Theodore Hsi-en Chen; "The Madness of Revolution," by Stefan Possony; "A Historical Study of the Chinese Communist Conflict in the Literature and Art of the Thirties," by Hsuan Meh; "Wu Han's Historical Viewpoint,"

18

by Li Yu-ning; and "The Chinese Communists' Policy Toward Intellectuals," by Wang Chang-ling.

Collected Works of Liu Shao-ch'i Before 1944. Hong Kong: Union Research Institute, 1969. 471 pp.

Collected Works of Liu Shao-ch'i, 1945-1957. Hong Kong: Union Research Institute, 1969. 484 pp.

Collected Works of Liu Shao-ch'i, 1958-1967. Hong Kong: Union Research Institute, 1968. 405 pp.

The above 3 titles comprise a total of 143 documents, including "self-examinations," by Liu Shao-ch'i, who was revealed as the archenemy of Mao Tse-tung and exposed during the Great Proletarian Cultural Revolution. Introduction by Chang Kuo-t'ao, one of the founders of the CCP.

Communist China, 1966. 2 vols. Hong Kong: Union Research Institute, 1968. 251 + 282 pp.

This 1966 Yearbook of Communist China includes the following analytical articles: "Literature and Art in Communist China, 1966," by Chao Ts'ung (Vol. II, pp. 1-43); "Education in Communist China, 1966," by Fang Cheng (Vol. II, pp. 44-86); "The Great Proletarian Cultural Revolution," by Chin Szu-kai (Vol. II, pp. 87-117); "Criticism of Academic Theories in Communist China, 1966," by Chung Wah-min (Vol. II, pp. 118-150); "Communist China's Science Work in 1966," by Chiu Shih-chih (Vol. II, pp. 151-170), and other related articles.

Communist China, 1967. 2 vols. Hong Kong: Union Research Institute, 1969. 329 + 266 pp.

Includes the following analytical articles: "The Great Proletarian Cultural Revolution in 1967," by Chung Hua-min (Vol. I, pp. 1-93); "Communist China's Cultural Work in

19

1967," by Chao Ts'ung (Vol. II, pp. 154-190); "Mainland China's Education in 1967," by Fang Cheng (Vol. II, pp. 191-226), and other related articles.

Communist China, 1968. Hong Kong: Union Research Institute, 1969. 499 pp.

Includes the following analytical articles: "The Great Proletarian Cultural Revolution in 1968," by Chang Man (pp. 5-68); "Education in Communist China, 1968," by Hsüeh Yu (pp. 427-458); "Cultural Work in Communist China," by Chung Hua-min (pp. 459-499), and other related articles.

Current Background. "Collection of Documents Concerning the Great Proletarian Cultural Revolution." No. 852 (May 6, 1968), 1-136.

The entire issue devoted to translations of 91 decisions, notifications, circulars, letters, and other documents issued by the CCP Central Committee, the State Council, the Military Commission of the Central Committee, the Cultural Revolution Group Under the Central Committee, and the CCP Peking Municipal Committee from May 16, 1966, through July 13, 1967.

————. "The Press Campaign Against Wu Han." No. 783 (March 21, 1966), 1-63.

Contents: "On the New Historical Play Dismissal of Hai Jui," by Yao Wen-yüan; "A Summary of Views on Dismissal of Hai Jui"; "Also on Hai Jui and the Dismissal of Hai Jui," by Ch'iao Tzu; "Self-Criticism on Dismissal of Hai Jui," by Wu Han; "Some Personages from Academic Circles in Shanghai Discuss Wu Han's 'Self-Criticism on Dismissal of Hai Jui.'"

————. "Revolution in Education." No. 846 (February 8, 1968), 1-56.

20

The entire issue devoted to translations of 16 reports and articles, in chronological order, showing the development of the revolution in education. A list of 55 titles of other articles and reports on educational reform is appended.

————. "Teng T'o, His 'Evening Talks at Yenshan' and the 'Three-Family Village' Group." No. 792 (June 29, 1966), 1-73.

A collection of press accounts documenting the case against Teng T'o. Contents: "Teng T'o's 'Evening Talks at Yenshan' Are Shady Articles Against the Party and Socialism," by Lin Hsieh and others; "On 'Three-Family Village,'" by Yao Wen-yüan; "Teng T'o — Big Conspirator Against the Party and Socialism," by Hsiao Chien and others; "Pei-ching wen-i Is a Branch of the 'Three-Family Village' Shady Inn," by Yin Wen-hsin and others; "Ch'ien-hsien — A Tool for Restoring Capitalism," by Liu Ch'eng-chieh.

FAN, K. H., ed. The Chinese Cultural Revolution: Selected Documents. New York: Grove Press, 1968. 320 pp.

A sparse collection of documents from Chinese Communist sources from 1939 to 1967, with an introductory note in each section by the editor.

Far Eastern Economic Review. "China 1968: Sketches from the Cultural Revolution." 62 (October 3, 1968), 74-75.

Contains four selected extracts of documents produced during the Great Proletarian Cultural Revolution.

FINCHER, John. "Mao's China: Old Images and New Reflections — Thirteen Books on China, Her Policies and Politics, in Review." Current Scene, 5 (March 31, 1967), 1-12.

Fraser, Stewart E., ed. Education and Communism in China: An Anthology of Commentary and Documents. London: Pall Mall Press, 1971. 614 pp.

A collection of 20 articles by foreign observers and scholars, the volume examines the full spectrum of education: primary schools, part-time and spare-time schooling, ideological education, scientific and technological education, international exchanges, and other aspects of Chinese education from the pre-1949 period to the Great Proletarian Cultural Revolution. In addition to the introductions to each of the nine sections, the editor also contributes two longer commentaries; a concluding chapter focuses on "Educational Developments Stemming from the Cultural Revolution," and 11 documents comprising major policy statements on education since the inception of the GPCR are appended.

Hsin pei-ta [New Peking University]. Chinese Communist Party, Central Committee. "(Draft) Provisions Concerning the Current GPCR in Institutions of Higher Learning (for Discussion and Trial Use)." March 14, 1967. Translated in Current Background, No. 846 (February 8, 1968).

Revolutionary teachers and students were ordered to return to their own campuses before March 20, 1967, to receive short-term military and political training. The formation of administrative organs and Red Guards was suggested.

HUANG, Chen-hsia. Chung-kung chün-jen chih [Chinese Communist Military Who's Who]. Hong Kong: Institute of Contemporary History, 1968. 823 pp.

This is the first biographical dictionary of leading Chinese Communist military officers and cadres published in book form outside China (PRC). It includes biographies of 726 military personalities, of whom 9 were marshals, 9 senior generals, 155 lieutenant generals, 280 major generals (these titles were used before the CCP abolished military ranks), and 216 cadres at divisional regimental and battalion levels, together with the "new dignitaries rising up" during the Great Proletarian Cultural Revolution.

22

Hung-ch'i [Red Flag]. "A New Type of School That Combines Theory with Practice." No. 4 (1968), 24-31. Translated in Chinese Education, 2 (Fall 1969), 15-27.

An investigative report on the Wukow Part-time Tea Growing and Part-time Study Middle School in Wuyuan County, Kiangsi Province.

Index to Selected Works of Mao Tse-tung. Hong Kong: Union Research Institute, 1968. 180 pp.

A detailed index to the proper nouns and terms in Selected Works of Mao Tse-tung, Vols. I to IV (Peking: Foreign Languages Press, 1965), and Selected Military Writing of Mao Tse-tung (Peking: Foreign Languages Press, 1963).

Index to Titles of English News Releases of Hsinhua News Agency, 1967. Hong Kong: Union Research Institute, 1968. 459 pp.

An index to proper nouns and terms in the titles of English Daily News Release published by Hsinhua News Agency, Hong Kong, in 1967. Titles are arranged chronologically.

KAO, Chung-yen. Chung-kung jen-shih pien-tung, 1959-1969 [Changes of Personnel in Communist China]. Hong Kong: Union Research Institute, 1970. 964 pp.

Covers senior personnel in the Party, army, and government at central and provincial levels from January 1959 to June 1969, based primarily on official news media from central and provincial levels, with a leavening of Red Guard newspapers and posters. Includes reports from Peking by Japanese correspondents gathering material on the Great Proletarian Cultural Revolution.

KLEIN, Donald W., and Anne B. Clark. Biographic Dictionary of Chinese Communists, 1921-1965. 2 vols. Cambridge, Mass.: Harvard University Press, 1971. 1194 pp.

Vol. I, Ai Szu-ch'i to Lo I-nung; Vol. II, Lo Jui-ch'ing

23

to Yun Tai-ying. This reference work provides biographies of 433 figures influential in the Chinese Communist Movement from the founding of the CCP in 1921 to 1965. Biographies include 200 Party Central Committee members, government ministers, provincial Party officials, military, labor, and youth leaders, scientists, artists, writers, and women. Ninety-six appendices integrate materials found in the text. Many of the figures involved in the Great Proletarian Cultural Revolution can be found in these two volumes.

LIU, Shao-ch'i. Quotations from President Liu Shao-ch'i. With an Introduction by C. P. Fitzgerald. Melbourne: Paul Flesch, 1968. 223 pp.

An English translation of the Chinese edition originally selected and published by Chih Luen Press, Hong Kong, in 1967. The quotations are selected from Liu Shao-ch'i's writings, reports, speeches, and other documents, from 1941 to 1966, and are arranged in 33 categories. Also included is an English text of the Constitution of the Chinese People's Republic and two biographical summaries concerning Liu Shao-ch'i's life up to 1968.

Long Live Victory of the Great Cultural Revolution Under the Dictatorship of the Proletariat. Peking: Foreign Languages Press, 1968. 49 pp.

This booklet consists of Lin Piao's speech at the Rally Celebrating the Eighteenth Anniversary of the Founding of the People's Republic of China on October 1, 1967; Chou En-lai's speech at the National Day Reception on September 30, 1967; "Long Live Victory of the Great Cultural Revolution Under the Dictatorship of the Proletariat," by the Editorial Departments of Jen-min jih-pao [People's Daily], Hung ch'i [Red Flag], and Chieh-fang-chün pao [Liberation Army Daily] on October 1, 1967; "A Great Revolution to Achieve the Ascendancy of Mao Tse-tung's Thought," editorial of Hung ch'i, No. 15 (1967); " 'Fight Self,

24

Repudiate Revisionism' Is the Fundamental Principle of the Great Proletarian Cultural Revolution," editorial of Jen-min jih-pao, October 6, 1967; and "To Repudiate Revisionism, It is Essential to Fight Self," editorial of Chieh-fang-chün pao, October 8, 1967.

MAO, Tse-tung. "Chairman Mao on Revolution in Education." Translated in Current Background, No. 888 (August 22, 1969), 1-20.

The entire issue contains translations of excerpts from Mao Tse-tung's writing on revolution in education during the period 1927 to 1967 arranged in chronological order. The original Chinese edition was first published by People's Publishing House, Peking, in 1967, and reprinted in Kwangtung in April 1969 for internal circulation.

———. "Chairman Mao Tse-tung's March 7 Directive Concerning the Great Strategic Plan for the Great Proletarian Cultural Revolution." Jen-min jih-pao [People's Daily], March 8, 1968. Translated in Chinese Education, 1 (Summer 1968), 61-62.

An English translation of the "March 7" Directive in which Mao called for the "three-in-one" combination.

———. "Mao Tse-tung Comments on Educational Reform." Issues & Studies, 6 (January 1970), 79-86.

Consists of 10 commentaries on educational reform excerpted from documents attributed to Mao Tse-tung before and during the Great Proletarian Cultural Revolution.

———. "Mao Tse-tung's Instructions Concerning the Great Proletarian Cultural Revolution." Translated in Current Background, No. 885 (July 31, 1969), 1-48.

Contains translations of excerpts of Mao Tse-tung's instructions concerning the Great Proletarian Cultural

25

Revolution appearing in major Chinese Communist newspapers from May 1966 to June 1968.

————. Mao Tse-tung's Quotations: The Red Guard's Handbook. Introduction by Stewart E. Fraser. Nashville, Tenn.: Peabody International Center, George Peabody College for Teachers, 1967. 312 pp.

This is an enlarged facsimile reproduction of the first English edition of Quotations from Chairman Mao Tsetung originally published by Foreign Languages Press, Peking, 1966, with an introduction added by Stewart E. Fraser on the origination of the Quotations and its important place in the Great Proletarian Cultural Revolution.

————. On Revolution and War. Edited with an Introduction and Notes by M. Rejai. Garden City, New York: Doubleday, 1969. 355 pp.

In this collection of Mao Tse-tung's essays, the editor offers an introduction to the thoughts of Mao Tse-tung for the general reader and also contributes capsule notes to each chapter. The excerpts are thematically grouped into chapters on imperialism, revolutionary development, united front tactics, global policies, and the respective roles of the Party and military.

————. The Political Thought of Mao Tse-tung. Selected and edited by Stuart R. Schram. Enl. & rev. ed. Harmondsworth, England: Penguin, 1969. 479 pp.

An anthology of passages commencing with Mao's first appearance in print, in 1919, down to his directives on the Great Proletarian Cultural Revolution, in 1966-1969.

————. Serve the People. In Memory of Norman Bethune. The Foolish Old Man Who Removed the Mountains. Peking: Foreign Languages Press, 1967. 11 pp.

26

The so-called "three constantly read articles." A major textbook used in schools and colleges during the Great Proletarian Cultural Revolution.

Min-kuo wu-shih-ch'i nien ti-ching ta-shih chi [Headline Events of the Chinese Communist Regime in 1968]. Taipei: Institute of Studies on Chinese Communist Affairs, National War College, 1969. 123 pp.

A chronicle of the important events which occurred in China for that year and international events closely related to the Chinese Communist government. The format consists of three parallel columns juxtaposing the affairs of the Chinese Communists, the USSR and other countries in the Communist bloc, and the international scene as a whole.

1967 Fei-ch'ing nien-pao [1967 Yearbook on Chinese Communism]. Taipei: Institute for the Study of Chinese Communist Problems, 1967. 1958 pp.

A comprehensive yearbook on Chinese Communism including sections on "The Great Proletarian Cultural Revolution" (pp. 235-366); "The Red Guard Movement" (pp. 677-686); "Culture and Education" (pp. 1243-1358); "Important Events in Communist China, 1966: Culture and Education" (pp. 1834-1856), and other related documents.

1968 Fei-ch'ing nien-pao [1968 Yearbook on Chinese Communism]. Taipei: Institute for the Study of Chinese Communist Problems, 1968. 1102 pp.

Including sections on "The Developments of the Cultural Revolution and Mainland Situation under the Cultural Revolution Tempest" (pp. 54-68); "Culture and Education in 1967" (pp. 188-213); "Original Materials on Cultural Revolution" (pp. 749-919); "Important Events in 1967: Cultural and Educational Affairs" (pp. 1032-1043), and other related documents.

27

1969 Chung-kung nien-pao [1969 Yearbook on Chinese Communism]. 2 vols. Taipei: Institute for the Study of Chinese Communist Problems, 1969. 1700 pp.

Including sections on "Chinese Communist Cultural and Educational Affairs in 1968" (Chapter II, pp. 122-188); "Changes in the Central Cultural Revolutionary Team and the Military Cultural Revolutionary Team" (Chapter III, pp. 1-9); "The Rise and Fall of the 'Red Guards'" (Chapter III, pp. 16-36); "Repercussions of the Chinese Communists 'Great Cultural Revolution'" (Chapter IV, pp. 1-106); "Important Documents: Cultural and Educational Affairs" (Chapter VII, pp. 56-70), and other related materials. [See explanatory note No. 4 in the Introduction.]

OKSENBERG, Michel C. A Bibliography of Secondary English Language Literature on Contemporary Chinese Politics. New York: East Asian Institute, Columbia University, 1970.

Peking Review. "Workers' Mao Tse-tung's Thought Propaganda Teams in Colleges and Schools." No. 43 (October 25, 1968). 13-16.

TENG, T'o. Yen-shan yeh-hua hsüan-chi [Selections from Evening Chats at Yenshan]. Hong Kong: Chih Luen Press, 1966. 157 pp.

Includes 45 essays originally published in Pei-ching wanpao [Peking Evening News], 1961-1962. The work was attacked as an "anti-Party, antisocialist black talk" early during the Great Proletarian Cultural Revolution.

TING, Wang, ed. Pei-ching shih wen-hua ta-ke-ming yün-tung [The Great Cultural Revolution Movement in Peking City]. Hong Kong: Ming Pao Monthly, 1970. 688 pp.

No. 5 of the series Chung-kung wen-hua ta-ke-ming tzu-liao

28

hui-pien [Documents of the Great Cultural Revolution in Communist China]. A collection of documents relating to Peking City issued by the CCP, speeches of Cultural Revolution leaders, documents from the old Municipal Committee of the CCP and the new Municipal Committee of CCP, documents issued by the Revolutionary Committee of Peking, and editorials from major newspapers related to Peking City.

————, ed. P'eng Te-huai wen-t'i chuan-chi [Special Collection on the Case of P'eng Te-huai]. Hong Kong: Ming Pao Monthly, 1969. 510 pp.

No. 3 of the series Chung-kung wen-hua ta-ke-ming tzu-liao hui-pien [Documents of the Great Cultural Revolution in Communist China]. A collection of documents by and about P'eng Te-huai; biograghical essays on P'eng Te-huai published prior to the Great Proletarian Cultural Revolution; press campaign against P'eng Te-huai; and articles and plays on Hai Jui.

————, ed. Teng T'o hsüan-chi [Selected Works of Teng T'o]. Hong Kong: Ming Pao Monthly, 1969. 582 pp.

No. 2 of the series Chung-kung wen-hua ta-ke-ming tzu-liao hui-pien [Documents of the Great Cultural Revolution in Communist China]. A collection of selected works of Teng T'o (including Yen-shan yeh-hua [Evening Chats at Yenshan]) and the press campaign against Teng T'o and his works. An index to Chinese Communist press articles against Teng T'o is appended.

————, ed. Tou-cheng chung-yang chi-kuan tang-ch'üan p'ai [Struggle Against the Clique in Authority in Central Organizations]. Hong Kong: Ming Pao Monthly, 1967. 717 pp.

No. 1 of the series Chung-kung wen-hua ta-ke-ming tzu-liao hui-pien [Documents of the Great Cultural Revolution in Communist China]. It includes four types of documents: documents from central organizations; important

editorials from major newspapers; important speeches
of central leading cadres; press campaign against the
"clique in authority": Liu Shao-ch'i, Teng Hsiao-p'ing,
T'ao Chu, Chu Te, Ch'en I, P'eng Chen, Lu T'ing-i, etc.

——, ed. Wu Han yü "Hai Jui pa-kuan" shih-chien [Wu Han
and the Affair of "Dismissal of Hai Jui"]. Hong Kong:
Ming Pao Monthly, 1969. 750 pp.

No. 4 of the series Chung-kung wen-hua ta-ke-ming tzu-
liao hui-pien [Documents of the Great Cultural Revolution
in Communist China]. It covers selected works of Wu Han
(the text of Dismissal of Hai Jui is not included) and the
press campaign against Wu Han and his play Dismissal of
Hai Jui (with few articles defending Wu). An index to Chinese Communist press articles against Wu Han is appended.

WANG, Hsueh-wen. Chung-kung wen-hua ta-ke-ming yü hung-
wei-ping [Chinese Communist Great Cultural Revolution
and the Red Guards]. Taipei: Institute of International
Relations, 1969. 734 pp.

Account of the Red Guard movement during the Great Proletarian Cultural Revolution. The chapters comprise such
topics as the organization of the Red Guards, their nature
and form; functions of the factions; the Red Guards' policy
of "break and foster" and the mutual impact between the
Red Guards and society; the big character wall posters;
the great alliance and great unity; export of Red Guards;
the Red Guards and education; internal conflicts and armed
struggle of the Red Guards; appraisal of the Red Guards, etc.

Who's Who in Communist China. 2 vols. Rev. ed. Hong Kong:
Union Research Institute, 1969. 522 + 402 pp.

Contains 2,837 names arranged according to romanized
spelling, with index of names arranged by stroke count.
Appendices on the CCP Ninth Central Committee, the provincial revolutionary committees, the military and

30

governmental personnel. Introduction by A. Doak Barnett. Termination date is September 5, 1968, for Volume I, and May 1, 1969, for Volume II.

WONG, Sybil. Dictionary of Chinese Communist Agricultural Terminology. Hong Kong: Union Research Institute, 1968. 572 pp.

Over 20,000 entries, with some 200 illustrations of terms selected from official Chinese Communist publications in the files of the Union Research Institute, Hong Kong, pertaining to all facets of Chinese agriculture, including plant pathology, farm machinery, political terminology, agronomy, etc. Characters arranged according to romanized spelling with index showing characters arranged by stroke count.

See also:

CHIEN, Yu-shen. China's Fading Revolution: Army Dissent and Military Divisions, 1967-68. Hong Kong: Center of Contemporary Chinese Studies, 1969. 405 pp. [III]

CHUANG, H. C. The Great Proletarian Cultural Revolution: A Terminological Study. Berkeley: Center for Chinese Studies, University of California, 1967. 72 pp. [III]

————. The Little Red Book and Current Chinese Language. Berkeley: Center for Chinese Studies, University of California, 1968. 58 pp. [III]

GRAY, Jack, and Patrick Cavendish. Chinese Communism in Crisis: Maoism and the Cultural Revolution. New York: Frederick A. Praeger, 1968. 279 pp. [III]

The Great Cultural Revolution in China. Compiled and edited

by the Asia Research Center. Melbourne & Sydney: Paul
Flesch and Co., 1968. 507 pp. [III]

The Great Power Struggle in China. Hong Kong: Asia Research
Center, 1969. 503 pp. [III]

The Great Socialist Cultural Revolution in China. 10 vols.
Peking: Foreign Languages Press, 1966-67. [III]

Great Victory for Chairman Mao's Revolutionary Line. Peking:
Foreign Languages Press, 1967. 88 pp. [III]

SCHICKEL, Joachim, ed. Mao Tse-tung: Der Grosse Strategische Plan. Dokumente zur Kulturrevolution. Berlin:
Edition Voltaire, 1969. 583 pp. [XIV]

YAO, Wen-yüan. The Working Class Must Exercise Leadership in Everything. Peking: Foreign Languages Press,
1968. 21 pp. Originally appeared in Hung-ch'i [Red Flag] ,
No. 2 (1968). Also translated in Selections from China
Mainland Magazines, No. 625 (September 3, 1968), 1-5. [III]

II. General survey and background

Asia. "Mainland China in the 1970's." 18 (Spring 1970), 16-36.

A summary of a panel discussion of a one-day conference sponsored by the Johnson Foundation and the Asia Society in June 1970 at Racine, Wisconsin. The Great Proletarian Cultural Revolution was one of the main topics discussed. The panelists were Edward Friedman, Melvin Gurtov, Victor Li, Dwight Perkins, and Ezra Vogel.

BARNETT, A. Doak. Cadres, Bureaucracy, and Political Power in Communist China. New York: Columbia University Press, 1967. 563 pp.

Describes the operative political system in China (PRC), where the "mass line" has necessitated that the Party rely on a large segment of society to carry out its campaigns to achieve specific national goals. The complex functions of ideological fervor, the suitability of propaganda, and the role of mass persuasion are also discussed.

————, ed. Chinese Communist Politics in Action. Seattle: University of Washington Press, 1969. 621 pp.

Twelve contributors discuss a wide range of topics, primarily related to personality and behavioral characteristics of leadership at the local and national levels. One article, entitled, "Sources and Methodological Problems in the Study of Contemporary China," recounts in detail the nature of contemporary Chinese research materials

34

available to the public at large.

BAUM, Richard. Ssu-Ch'ing: The Socialist Education Movement of 1962-1966. Berkeley: University of California, 1968. 126 pp.

BUSH, Richard C., Jr. Religion in Communist China. Nashville, Tenn.: Abingdon Press, 1970. 432 pp.

Concentrating on Christianity in China, the author also deals with other major religious forces of pre-Communist China, namely Taoism, Confucianism, Buddhism, Islam; a comprehensive study of the scope of religious suppression based mainly on sources available from outside China.

CHAI, Winberg, ed. Essential Works of Chinese Communism. New York: Pica Press, 1970. 464 pp.

The editor presents in chronological order some 31 major works, beginning with the "First Manifesto of the Party Central Committee on the Situation in China in 1922" through some major works of Mao Tse-tung, Liu Shao-ch'i, Lin Piao, Teng Hsiao-p'ing, P'eng Chen and an editorial that appeared in Peking Review in July 1968.

CHEN, Nai Ruenn and Walter Galenson. Chinese Economy Under Communism. Chicago: Aldine Publishing Co., 1969. 250 pp.

The authors begin with an assessment of the economy in pre-Communist China, detail in a realistic manner what choices were open to the new government, and report what choices were made, including the failure of the Great Leap Forward policy. Subsequent policy decisions are also discussed. The rest of the work examines the specifics of industrialization, agriculture, reorganization of the economic decision-making process, conditions of life in China, foreign economic relations, and the prospects facing the economy in the future.

China News Analysis. "Policy or Rivalry? The Roots of the Cultural Revolution: The 1959 Lushan Meeting." No. 685 (November 17, 1967), 1-7.

Discusses the Lushan Meeting and the case of P'eng Te-huai and the motive behind the Great Proletarian Cultural Revolution.

CHUNG, Hua-min, and Arthur C. Miller. Madame Mao — A Profile of Chiang Ch'ing. Hong Kong: Union Research Institute, 1968. 320 pp.

An English edition of Chiang Ch'ing chen chuan [A Biography of Chiang Ch'ing] published by the same publisher in 1967.

CROZIER, Ralph C., ed. China's Cultural Legacy and Communism. New York: Praeger, 1970. 313 pp.

DOUGLASS, Bruce, and Ross Terrill, eds. China and Ourselves: Explorations and Revisions by a New Generation. Preface by Edgar Snow. Boston: Beacon Press, 1971. 259 pp.

Contents: "China Visited: A View of the Cultural Revolution," Stephen Fitzgerald; "The Meaning of the Cultural Revolution," Ray Wylie; "China's Special Modernity," Jon Saari; "China and the Unfinished Revolution of Asia," Feliciano Carion; "Long Day's Journey: American Observers in China, 1948-50," Tom Engelhardt; "John Carter Vincent and the American 'Loss' of China," Ross Terrill; "Peking and Washington: Is Taiwan the Obstacle?" Edward Friedman; "The Good Earth and the Good Society," Neale Hunter; "The Long March and the Exodus: 'The Thought of Mao Tse-tung' and the Contemporary Significance of 'Emissary Prophecy'," Kazuhiko Sumiya; "The Socialist Tradition and China's New Socialism," Bruce Douglass.

DOW, Thomas E., Jr. "The Population of China." Current

36

History, 55 (September 1968), 141-146.

Analyzes the population trends in China based on the 1953 census and estimates population growth between 1953 and 1968 with a discussion on the population policy and population control in the future.

GRAY, Jack, ed. Modern China's Search for a Political Form. New York: Oxford University Press, 1969. 379 pp.

This symposium contains 10 essays examining modern Chinese political development, with an emphasis on the Communist revolution, contributed by a group of specialists, government officials, and journalists; this volume begins with the historical antecedents of the Chinese revolution and concludes with speculation about the Great Proletarian Cultural Revolution.

HO, Ping-ti, and Tang Tsou, eds. China in Crisis. 2 vols. in 3. With a Forward by Charles U. Daly. Chicago: University of Chicago Press, 1968. 803 + 484 pp.

Papers presented at two five-day conferences in February 1967 at the University of Chicago. Volume I, Books 1 and 2, on "China's Heritage and the Communist Political System"; Volume II on "China's Politics in Asia and America's Alternatives." The 3 volumes include 13 major studies by various scholars. Most studies include commentaries by specialists. The authors attempt to explain the philosophical, institutional, economic, and sociological foundations of Communist China. Two chapters are specifically devoted to the Great Proletarian Cultural Revolution: "Cultural Revolution and Revisionism," by C. K. Yang; and "The Attack of the Cultural Revolution in Ideology and Organization," by Franz Schurmann.

LEWIS, John W., ed. The City in Communist China. Stanford, Calif.: Stanford University Press, 1971. 370 pp.

The first of three volumes on the Chinese city, this volume examines the city as it exists in Communist China; the other two volumes will study the city as it existed in late Imperial China and during the days of the Republic. A collection of papers most of which were originally presented at a conference held under the joint auspices of the Social Science Research Council and the American Council of Learned Societies, the separate chapters deal with the problems of law and order, leadership and bureaucracy, modernization and China's urban crisis.

Party Leadership and Revolutionary Power in China. New York: Cambridge University Press, 1970. 422 pp.

Consists of 11 papers presented at a conference on the Chinese Communist Party held in England in July 1968, with an introduction by the editor. It begins with an account of Mao's rise to power and his changing concept of Party morality, followed by an examination of the Communist ideology, Party motivation, and elite factionalism, and their effect on Chinese society after 1949. The final chapters concern the power struggle between the central government and village leaders and illustrate the role which the army played during the Great Proletarian Cultural Revolution.

LI, Tien-min. Chou En-lai. Taipei: Institute of International Relations, 1970. 426 pp.

A biographical study of Chou En-lai of which three chapters are devoted to Chou's performance during the more than two decades of his premiership. Chou En-lai's role during the Great Proletarian Cultural Revolution is traced through the use of original materials. The last chapter, "Chou's Profile and His Future," covers an analysis of the interrelations among Mao Tse-tung, Liu Shao-ch'i, Lin Piao, and Chou En-lai and a prediction concerning Chou's political future.

38

LI, Ting-sheng. The CCP's Persecution of Chinese Intellectuals in 1949-69. Taipei: Asian People's Anti-Communist League, 1969. 67 pp.

The author first traces the history of discrimination against intellectuals by the Chinese Communists. In the first part of the book, the author enumerates examples of incidents of repression of intellectuals before the Great Proletarian Cultural Revolution. Then the purges and "re-education" campaign during the GPCR are discussed. The author concludes that Mao will never be able to transform the intellectuals into docile tools and they will continue to play a significant role in the political development of China (PRC).

MEHNERT, Klaus. "Mao and Maoism: Some Soviet Views." Current Scene, 8 (September 1, 1970), 1-16.

Reviews how Soviet writers deal with Maoism in USSR literary publications.

MELBY, John F., ed. Contemporary China. Toronto: The Canadian Institute of International Affairs, 1968. 138 pp.

This book deals with a range of problems of immediate relevance to China's domestic and external political development. C. H. G. Oldham's article on "Science and Technology in China's Future" elaborates on the national goals which China's leaders sense they must achieve if their country is to be converted from a tradition-bound society to a modernizing one.

MYERS, James T. "The Fall of Chairman Mao." Current Scene, 6 (June 15, 1968), 1-18.

"This article seeks to explore the background of civil strife and disorder and to determine what role may be assigned to the Great Leader, Great Teacher, Great Helmsman, Great Supreme Commander Mao Tse-tung in the

39

breakdown of civilian authority and the threatened disintegration of the Chinese revolution."

NASHIMOTO, Yuhei. Chou En-lai. Tokyo: Keiso Shokyoku, 1967.

This book in Japanese consists of eight chapters: Early Life, Appearance on the Political Stage; Increasing Activity; Association with Chiang Kai-shek; Era of Civil War; Voice of Asia; Problem Concerning Japan; and the Great Proletarian Cultural Revolution. A chronological list of Chou's participation in the major events of the CCP is appended at the end of the book.

NEUHAUSER, Charles. "The Chinese Communist Party in the 1960's: Prelude to the Cultural Revolution." The China Quarterly, No. 32 (October-December 1967), 3-36.

OKSENBERG, Michel. "The Institutionalization of the Chinese Communist Revolution: The Ladder of Success on the Eve of the Cultural Revolution." The China Quarterly, No. 36 (October-December 1968), 61-92.

Problems of Communism. "China in Flux." 18 (November-December 1969), 1-14.

Contains four articles. Parris H. Chang, in his article "The Second Decade of Maoist Rule," surveys the record of the last years, examines the makeup of the new leadership installed at the Ninth CCP Congress of April 1969, and endeavors to assess the probable direction of its policies. In "The Pursuit of Purity: Mao's Cultural Revolution," Richard M. Pfeffer presents an interpretation of that movement, seeing it as an attempt by Mao to fuse "explosive idealism and intense power" in a struggle to preserve his own vision of the goal of the Chinese Communist Revolution. In "The New Role of the Military," Stephen A. Sims focuses on the enhanced role of the military in the

40

government of China and the potentialities of the People's Liberation Army for filling that role. Maury Lisann, in "Moscow and the Chinese Power Struggle," offers an analysis of Soviet attempts to influence the course of the power struggle between Mao and his opponents in the Great Proletarian Cultural Revolution, and shows Moscow's inclination to intervene in support of pro-Soviet elements in China.

PRYBYLA, Jan S. "China's Economy: Experiments in Maoism." Current History, 59 (September 1970), 159-164.

―――. "Communist China: The Economy and the Revolution." Current History, 55 (September 1968), 135-140.

PYE, Lucian. The Spirit of Chinese Politics. Cambridge, Mass.: Massachusetts Institute of Technology, 1968. 255 pp.

In a wide-ranging series of essays, the author investigates the Chinese personality in terms of a broad spectrum of psychological forces impinging upon individuals in their total social environment. The book shows that the Chinese have their own special models for understanding the world around them and their place in it.

SCHURMANN, Herbert Franz. Ideology and Organization in Communist China. 2d ed. Berkeley: University of California Press, 1968. 642 pp.

Analyzes the organization of the Party, the role of ideology, and the methods of management and administration. This new edition is a reprint of the 1966 edition with some minor corrections and includes a 90-page supplement bringing it up to date.

SCHWARTZ, Benjamin I. Communism and China: Ideology in Flux. Cambridge, Mass.: Harvard University Press, 1968. 254 pp.

A collection of essays on Chinese Communism written by the author between 1954 and 1967, including an essay entitled "Upheaval in China (1967)" which discusses briefly the Great Proletarian Cultural Revolution. The essay was first published in Commentary, February 1967.

SEYBOLT, Peter J. "Yenan Education and the Chinese Revolution, 1937-1945." Unpublished Ph.D. Dissertation, Harvard University, 1969. 440 pp.

This study examines the origins of many Cultural Revolution education policies.

SOLOMON, Richard H. "The Pattern of the Chinese Revolution." Current History, 55 (September 1968), 129-134.

Discusses the current leadership crisis in Communist China and traces how "natural disaster, the ravages of local warlords and the accumulated resentments of landlord exploitation exposed for Mao the key to the 'boundless energy of the masses'...which, once liberated, could make the peasants a revolutionary force."

SPITZ, Allen A., ed. Contemporary China. Pullman, Washington: Washington State University, 1967. 56 pp.

Five papers selected from the contributions made at the World Affairs Institute on Contemporary China, Washington State University, on March 30-31, 1967, including "Communist China's Economic Prospects and the Cultural Revolution" by Yuan-li Wu (pp. 33-42).

TOWNSEND, James R. Political Participation in Communist China. Berkeley: University of California Press, 1969. 233 pp.

Describes the overall nature of the Chinese Communist system, including Party restraints on the electoral

42

process through propaganda campaigns, the selection and training of cadres, and the management of legal organizations, such as congresses and people's tribunals. The author studies both concepts and practices of political participation by the masses in their legal organizations. Attention is given to the methods whereby the peasants are prepared psychologically to participate in small group discussions, criticisms, and decisions.

U.S. Department of State. Communist China. Washington, D.C.: U.S. Government Printing Office, 1969. 32 pp.

This pamphlet is No. 4 of the "Issues Series" issued by the U.S. Department of State. It summarizes current information about China and raises relevant questions as an aid to public discussion of the important issues in United States foreign policy. It includes a short section on the Great Proletarian Cultural Revolution, its aftermath, and some notes on education.

VOGEL, Ezra F. Canton Under Communism: Programs and Politics in a Provincial Capital, 1949-1968. Cambridge, Mass.: Harvard University Press, 1969. 448 pp.

The history, dynamics, and realities of Chinese life and politics as reflected in one region, Canton, are comprehensively described, based primarily on newspapers, reports of foreign travelers and refugees, and printed works from Canton, as well as sources outside China.

WANG, Chang-ling. Chung-kung ti wen-i cheng-feng [Chinese Communist Rectification in Literature and Art Fields]. Taipei: Institute of International Relations, 1967. 264 pp.

Gives a brief account of the major rectification campaigns in the literature and art fields of the Chinese Communists from the Yenan period up to early 1967, the early phase of the Great Proletarian Cultural Revolution. It begins with the purge of Wang Shih-wei in 1942 for his article "Wild Lily" and ends with the case of Teng T'o, Wu Han, and Liao Mo-sha. The book also devotes a whole chapter to a general analysis of the meaning, factors, and background of the persecution.

WU, Chun-hsi. Dollars, Dependents and Dogma. Introduction by C. F. Remer. Stanford, Calif.: Hoover Institution on War, Revolution, and Peace, 1967. 237 pp.

Deals with the important question of overseas Chinese remittances to China (PRC), including a discussion on the shrinkage of funds available in the last few years resulting from the Great Proletarian Cultural Revolution and other causes.

YIN, Ching-yao. Li-shih hsieh hsia liao ta-an: Kung-ch'an-tang hsuan-yen i-erh-ling nien [History Has Given the Answer: 120 Years After the Communist Manifesto]. Taipei: Jointly Published by the Institute of International Relations and the Institute of East Asian Studies, National Chengchi University, 1968. 552 pp.

Consists of three parts: Part I discusses fundamental Communist doctrines and theories; Part II assesses economic development in noncommunist nations; Part III, on the practice of Communism and its problems.

See also:

The Case of P'eng Teh-huai, 1959-1968. Hong Kong: Union Research Institute, 1968. 515 pp. [I]

CHUANG, H. C. Evening Chats at Yenshan, or the Case of Teng T'o. Berkeley: Center for Chinese Studies, University of California, 1970. 46 pp. [III]

44

Collected Documents of the First Sino-American Conference on Mainland China. Taipei: Institute of International Relations, 1971. 951 pp. [I]

Collected Works of Liu Shao-ch'i Before 1944. Hong Kong: Union Research Institute, 1969. 471 pp. [I]

Collected Works of Liu Shao-ch'i, 1945-1957. Hong Kong: Union Research Institute, 1969. 484 pp. [I]

Collected Works of Liu Shao-ch'i, 1958-1967. Hong Kong: Union Research Institute, 1968. 405 pp. [I]

HSIAO, Gene T. "The Background and Development of 'The Proletarian Cultural Revolution.'" Asian Survey, 7 (June 1967), 389-404. [III]

HSIUNG, V. T. Red China's Cultural Revolution. New York: Vantage Press, 1968. 188 pp. [III]

Kung-fei li-tz'u wen-i cheng-feng chen-hsiang [The Chinese Communists' Successive Rectifications in Literary and Art Fields]. Taipei: The Sixth Division of the Kuomintang Central Committee, 1970. 365 pp. [III]

Problems of Communism. "More on Maoism." 16 (March-April 1967), 91-99. [III]

————. "What Is Maoism? A Symposium." 15 (September-October 1966), 1-30. [III]

TENG, T'o. Yen-shan yeh-hua hsüan-tsi [Selections from Evening Chats at Yenshan] Hong Kong: Chih Luen Press, 1966. 157 pp. [I]

III. Great Proletarian Cultural Revolution

ANDO, Hikotaro. Bunka daikakumei no kenkyu [Studies of the Great Cultural Revolution]. Tokyo: Aki Shoten, 1968. 208 pp.

ASAMI, Kazuo. Bunka daikakumei juni no gimon [Twelve Questions of the Great Cultural Revolution]. Tokyo: Shinko Shoten, 1967. 294 pp.

BARCATA, Louis. China in the Throes of the Cultural Revolution: An Eye Witness Report. New York: Hart Publishing Company, 1967. 299 pp.

Based on a visit to the People's Republic in the spring of 1967, the author reports in words and pictures on the events, progress, and prospects of the Great Proletarian Cultural Revolution and offers some interpretations of these events.

BAUM, Richard. "China: Year of the Mangoes." Asian Survey, 9 (January 1969), 1-17.

―――. "The Cultural Revolution: A Parting of Paupers." Far Eastern Economic Review, 59 (January 4, 1968), 17-19.

The author analyzes the development of rival factions led by Wang Kuo-fan, commune director of the "paupers' co-op" in Hopei Province, and Tu Kuei, head of Hsipu Brigade of the "paupers' co-op."

―――. "Revolution and Reaction in the Chinese Countryside:

46

The Socialist Education Movement in Cultural Revolutionary Perspective." The China Quarterly, No. 38 (April-June 1969), 92-119.

————, and Frederick C. Teiwes. "Liu Shao-ch'i and the Cadre Question." Asian Survey, 8 (April 1968), 323-345.

————, and Louise B. Bennett, eds. China in Ferment: Perspectives on the Cultural Revolution. Englewood Cliffs, New Jersey: Prentice-Hall, 1971. 246 pp.

BENNETT, Gordon. "China's Continuing Revolution: Will It Be Permanent?" Asian Survey, 10 (January 1970), 2-17.

————. "Madam Mao's Polemicist Laureate: Mrs. Mao's Literary Ghost." Far Eastern Economic Review, 62 (October 24, 1968), 197-199.

An analysis of Yao Wen-yüan's writings and political career and his rise during the Great Proletarian Cultural Revolution.

BLUMER, Giovanni. Die Chinesische Kulturrevolution 1965/67. Frankfurt am Main: Europaische Verlagsanstalt, 1968. 399 pp.

BUGUNOVIC, Branko. "The Cultural Revolution: Too Good to Last." Far Eastern Economic Review, 59 (February 1, 1968), 195-198.

A Yugoslavian journalist who was expelled from China in March 1967 for "false and slanderous reports" discusses the Great Proletarian Cultural Revolution by looking back on his many years as a correspondent in Peking and analyzes the importance of "bourgeois tendencies" as a target of the movement and the losses which China has suffered as a result.

47

BRIDGHAM, Phillip. "Mao's Cultural Revolution in 1967: The Struggle to Seize Power." The China Quarterly, No. 34 (April-June 1966), 6-37.

————. "Mao's 'Culture Revolution': Origin and Development." The China Quarterly, No. 29 (January-March 1967), 1-35.

The author traces back to the Lushan meeting in 1959, when Mao's policy was attacked by P'eng Te-huai, then the retreat of Mao from 1961-62; the launching of socialist education; the rectification campaign on the front of literature and art; the call to criticize "bourgeois reactionary thinking"; the political attack on Wu Han; the creation of the Red Guards; and the prospects of the Great Proletarian Cultural Revolution.

————. "Mao's Cultural Revolution: The Struggle to Consolidate Power." The China Quarterly, No. 41 (January-March 1970), 1-25.

Carry the Great Revolution on the Journalistic Front Through to the End. Peking: Foreign Languages Press, 1969. 64 pp.

A joint editorial of Jen-min jih-pao [People's Daily], Hung-ch'i [Red Flag], and Chieh-fang-chün pao [Liberation Army Daily] "repudiating the counterrevolutionary revisionist line on journalism of China's Khrushchov."

"The Case of Wu Han in the Cultural Revolution (I)." Special issue of Chinese Studies in History and Philosophy, 2 (Fall 1968), 3-107.

The following articles are translated: Wu Han, "Preface [to The Dismissal of Hai Jui]" and "A Self-Criticism of The Dismissal of Hai Jui"; Yao Wen-yüan, "On the New Historical Play The Dismissal of Hai Jui"; "Letter from Four Comrades in the History Department of Fu Tan University"; Chu Hsi, "How to Evaluate The Dismissal of Hai

48

Jui"; Yen Jen, "Some Views on the Historical Play The Dismissal of Hai Jui."

"The Case of Wu Han in the Cultural Revolution (II)." Special issue of Chinese Studies in History and Philosophy, 2 (Spring 1969), 3-70.

The following articles are translated: Shih Wen-ch'ün, "Academic Circles of Wuhan Launch Discussions on The Dismissal of Hai Jui"; "Some Views on The Dismissal of Hai Jui Among Canton Academic Circles"; Wu Chün-wei, "There Were Differences Between Honest Officials and Corrupt Officials"; Shen Chih, "Hai Jui Should Be Both Criticized and Affirmed"; T'an Yüan-shou, "Improve Our Understanding Through Discussions on The Dismissal of Hai Jui"; Chi Hung-hsü, "'Honest Officials' Should Be Treated from a Class Viewpoint"; Shih Shao-pin, "Comments on 'A Self-Criticism of The Dismissal of Hai Jui'"; "A Group Discussion by Members of Shanghai Academic Circles on Wu Han's 'A Self-Criticism of The Dismissal of Hai Jui'"; Shih Han-jen, "Some Objections to Criticisms of The Dismissal of Hai Jui."

"The Case of Wu Han in the Cultural Revolution (III)." Special issue of Chinese Studies in History, 3 (Fall 1969), 3-85.

The following articles are translated: Ch'i Pen-yü, "The True Reactionary Nature of 'Hai Jui Scolds the Emperor' and The Dismissal of Hai Jui"; Shih Shao-pin, "Hu Shih and Wu Han"; Wang Cheng-p'ing, Ting Wei-chih, et al., "Comrade Wu Han's Anti-Party, Antisocialist, Anti-Marxist Political Thinking and Academic Viewpoints."

"The Case of Wu Han in the Cultural Revolution (IV)." Special issue of Chinese Studies in History, 3 (Winter 1969-70), 91-176.

The following articles are translated: "Polemics Regarding the Class Nature of Ethics and Their Inheritance"; Hsü

Ch'i-hsien, "Where Does the True Significance of the Theory of Mutual 'Acceptance' of Ethics by Opposite Classes Lie?"; Yung Chao-tsu, "On Inheritance of Ethics and on Language"; "May the Ethics of the Exploiting Classes be Critically Inherited?"; Lin Chieh, "On 'A Self-Criticism Regarding the Discussion on Ethics'"; Kuan Feng and Wu Ch'uan-chi, "Comments on Comrade Wu Han's Theory of Ethics"; Meng P'ei-yüan, "Opposition to Feudal Ethics During the May 4th Movement Was an Uncompromising Revolutionary Struggle."

"The Case of Wu Han in the Cultural Revolution (V)." Chinese Studies in History, 3 (Spring 1970), 179-223.

The following articles are translated: Ts'ai Shao-ching, Teng T'o Disseminates Poison at a Peking Daily Meeting"; "Irrefutable Proof that 'Three-Family Village' Poisons and Woos Young People"; Lin Chieh, "Expose Teng T'o's Anti-Party, Antisocialist Features"; Wu Tung-hui, "Smash the Black Backstage of 'Three-Family Village.'"

CHAI, Winberg. "The Reorganization of the Chinese Communist Party, 1966-1968." Asian Survey, 8 (November 1968), 901-910.

CHANG, Man. The People's Daily and the Red Flag Magazine During the Cultural Revolution. Hong Kong: Union Research Institute, 1969. 126 pp.

CHANG, Parris H. "Leadership Purges in China: The Fallen Idols." Far Eastern Economic Review, 61 (August 22, 1968), 351-353.

The author suggests that the purge of "capitalist-roaders" has been of much greater dimensions than was originally expected; from the Central Committee down to the provinces, the ranks of veteran Party leaders have been decimated.

50

————. "The Revolutionary Committee in China: Two Case Studies: Heilungkiang and Honan." Current Scene, 6 (June 1, 1968), 1-37.

————. "Struggle Between the Two Roads in China's Countryside." Current Scene, 6 (February 15, 1968), 1-14.

"This article surveys the major issues of contention within the Party about rural policies, identifying major participants and their different perspectives, and offers some observations on the problems encountered by the Party."

CHANG, Yao-ch'iu. Kung-fei "wen-hua ta ke-ming" ti p'ou-hsi [Analyses of the Chinese Communist Great Cultural Revolution]. Taipei: Commission of Overseas Chinese Affairs, 1966. 54 pp.

CHENG, Chu-yuan. "The Cultural Revolution and China's Economy." Current History, 53 (September 1967), 148-154.

Evaluation of China's economic problems with special attention to the impact and disruption of the Great Proletarian Cultural Revolution on the Chinese economy.

CH'I, Ming. Chung-kung wen-hua ke-ming chen-hsiang [The True Picture of Chinese Communist Cultural Revolution]. Hong Kong: Ping Chen Press, 1966. 60 pp.

Chiao-hsüeh p'i-p'an [Pedagogical Critique]. August 20, 1967, Published by the Editorial Committee of the Peking University Cultural Revolutionary Committee.

The issue contains "contributions by Red Guard groups in the Ministry of Higher Education" and at the time of publication was "the most comprehensive review of policy conflict in higher education." For a complete translation of this publication, see Chinese Sociology and Anthropology (Fall-Winter 1969-70), 124 pp. This issue contains the

51

following articles: "Supreme Directives"; A Commentator, "Thoroughly Destroy the Reactionary and Revisionist Educational Line of Liu [Shao-ch'i] and Teng [Hsiao-p'ing]"; The "Red Rock" Fighting Company, Peking Commune, Ministry of Higher Education; The "July 1" Fighting Company, Minister of Higher Education; The "Torch" Fighting Company, New Peking University Commune, "A Record of the Great Events in the Struggle Between the Two Lines in the Field of Higher Education"; Second Class of the Fifth Year Students, Department of Language and Literature, Peking University, "Unveiling the Dark Side of the Chinese Department's Professional Program in Classical Studies"; "Welcoming the New High Tide of the Great Educational Revolution"; "Educational Reform Activities in the Universities and Colleges"; Glossary.

Chieh-fang-chün pao [Liberation Army Daily]. "Hold High the Great Red Banner of Mao Tse-tung and Take an Active Part in the Great Socialist Cultural Revolution." April 18, 1966. Translated in Survey of China Mainland Press, No. 3687 (April 29, 1966), 4-15.

This Chieh-fang-chün pao editorial, reprinted next day by Jen-min jih-pao [People's Daily], was a declaration of war against "an anti-Party, anti-socialist black line in literature and art" that had been running counter to the thought of Mao Tse-tung. As the line followed by Party intellectuals under the wing of the Liu Shao-ch'i clique was both revisionist and capitalist, this editorial was in fact Lin Piao's declaration of war, calling all members of the army to eradicate his political rivals.

CHIEN, Yu-shen. China's Fading Revolution: Army Dissent and Military Divisions, 1967-68. Hong Kong: Center of Contemporary Chinese Studies, 1969. 405 pp.

This book is based upon a section of a larger work entitled Upheaval in China — The Great Proletarian Cultural

52

Revolution in Historical Perspective, 1966-69, which is yet to be published. This volume covers the violent phase of the Great Proletarian Cultural Revolution which began in mid-1967 at Wuhan and was declining by late 1968. The author presents an analysis of the events leading to army defiance of central authority at Wuhan and the violence which followed. A number of documents are appended, including press releases, speeches, and Party directives related to the text.

China After the Cultural Revolution: A Selection from the Bulletin of Atomic Scientists. New York: Vintage Books, 1970. 247 pp.

This volume, reprinted from the Bulletin of the Atomic Scientists, is divided into four parts: the political struggle in China; the economy; foreign policy; and science and technology. The collection includes twelve articles by authors such as C. P. Fitzgerald, Jack Gray, and John M. H. Lindbeck.

China News Analysis. "Cultural Revolution in Kwangtung: Part I: The First Year, Summer 1966-Spring 1967." No. 724 (September 6, 1968), 1-7.

————."Cultural Revolution in Kwangtung: Part II: The Second Year, Summer 1967-Summer 1968." No. 727 (October 4, 1968), 1-7.

————. "Cultural Revolution in Kwangtung: Part III: Summer and Autumn 1968." No. 728 (October 11, 1968), 1-7.

————. "What If the Cultural Revolution Succeeds?" No. 669 (July 21, 1967), 1-7.

————. "Wu Han and the Monk P'eng." No. 606 (April 1, 1966), 1-7.

The China Quarterly. "Foreign Expert." "Eyewitness of the
Cultural Revolution." No. 28 (October-December 1966), 1-7.

CHING, Shui-hsien. Rifle Rectifies Rifle in Mao's Cultural
Revolution. Taipei: Asian People's Anti-Communist
League, 1969. 75 pp.

Analyzes the cause and effect of rectification in the army
both before and during the Great Proletarian Cultural Revolution. It begins with a brief review of the various movements in the Communist army starting from 1953. The
author then discusses the role that the army has played in
rectifying the Party and state organizations during the
GPCR. A list of the senior military cadres purged during
the GPCR is appended at the end of the book.

CHUANG, H. C. Evening Chats at Yenshan, or the Case of
Teng T'o. Berkeley: Center for Chinese Studies, University of California, 1970. 46 pp.

Monograph No. 14 of the series "Studies in Chinese Communist Terminology." This study concerns the work of a
single figure, Teng T'o, one of the primary targets of the
attack upon the discontented Communist intellectuals during the Great Proletarian Cultural Revolution. The study
covers the career and downfall of Teng T'o, his "Evening
Chats at Yenshan," the criticism of him, and a glossary
of terms, names, and titles related to the case.

————. The Great Proletarian Cultural Revolution: A Terminological Study. Berkeley: Center for Chinese Studies, University of California, 1967. 72 pp.

Monograph No. 12 of the series "Studies in Chinese Communist Terminology." This study, as well as others in
this series, concerns the terminology used in the major
Chinese Communist sociopolitical movements which have
given rise to new terms, revived old vocabulary, or

54

generated new usages. The author traces in each case the
source of the term, not only for the academic interest of
linguistic history, but to gain insight into the character of
those who have directed the campaign.

―――. The Little Red Book and Current Chinese Language.
Berkeley: Center for Chinese Studies, University of California, 1968. 58 pp.

Monograph No. 13 of the series "Studies in Chinese Communist Terminology." The study attempts to focus attention on a few of the more salient linguistic points of the
Quotations from Chairman Mao Tse-tung. Employing a
semantic approach, the author examines various features
of Mao's style of writing and investigates the historical
origin of certain expressions.

Chung-kuo ch'ing-nien pao [China Youth News]. "Take a Look
at the Irrefutable Evidence of How 'Three-Family Village'
Harms and Woos Youths," May 14, 1966. Translated in
Survey of China Mainland Press, No. 3709 (June 1, 1966), 6-10.

Another report on Teng T'o's activities, defending Wu Han
as well as himself.

Current Background. "The Wicked History of Big Conspirator,
Big Ambitionist, Big Warlord P'eng Te-huai," No. 851
(April 16, 1968), 31 pp.

P'eng, predecessor of Lin Piao, was attacked by Red
Guards, who had compiled this booklet containing numerous
charges against P'eng, including his cordial relations
with Khrushchev.

DAY, Shen-yu. "Peking's 'Cultural Revolution.'" Current
History, 51 (September 1966), 134-139.

In analyzing the meaning of the "Cultural Revolution,"
the author traces what the Chinese Communists have been

55

trying to undertake in the 1960s and believes that "the leadership directing these events, over and above any question of internal differences, moved to show clearly that change, when it must come, must be in line with established policy and theory...."

Decision of the Central Committee of the Chinese Communist Party Concerning the Great Proletarian Cultural Revolution. Peking: Foreign Languages Press, 1966. 13 pp.

Text of the so-called "16-Point Decision" on the Great Proletarian Cultural Revolution adopted at the Eleventh Plenary Session of the Eighth Central Committee of the CCP on August 8, 1966.

DELIUSIN, Lev Petrovich. The "Cultural Revolution" in China. Moscow: Novosti Press Agency Publishing House, 1967, 103 pp.

A Soviet analysis of the Great Proletarian Cultural Revolution.

DEUTSCHER, Isaac. Deutscher on the Chinese Cultural Revolution. London: Bertrand Russell Peace Foundation, 1967. 15 pp.

The Diary of the Great Cultural Revolution: October '66- April '67. Tokyo: Asahi Evening News Co., Ltd., 1967.

DOMES, Jürgen. "The Cultural Revolution and the Army." Asian Survey, 8 (May 1968), 349-363.

DUTT, Gargi, and V. P. Dutt. China's Cultural Revolution. New York: Asia Publishing House, 1970. 260 pp.

The authors trace the background of the Great Proletarian Cultural Revolution back to the period of the Great Leap Forward. The analysis is then picked up with the hundred days of storm, the Shanghai January Revolution, the peak of the GPCR, and consolidation.

56

ELEGANT, Robert S. Mao's Great Revolution. New York:
World Publishing Co., 1971. 478 pp.

Report on the machinations of the inner circle of the Chinese Communist Party before, during, and after the Great
Proletarian Cultural Revolution. The author details the
crosscurrents that led to the Red Guard uprisings and to
the crushing of that Mao-inspired movement. He relates
how the army reestablished some degree of effective rule
while Mao was relegated to a weakened position.

FALKENHEIM, Victor C. "The Cultural Revolution in Kwangsi,
Yunnan and Fukien." Asian Survey, 9 (August 1969), 580-597.

FANN, K. T. "Philosophy in the Chinese Cultural Revolution."
International Philosophical Quarterly, 9 (September
1969), 449-459.

A paper presented at a symposium on "Marxism and Chinese Developments" sponsored by the Society for the Philosophical Study of Dialectical Materialism and held in conjunction with the 65th Annual Meeting of the American
Philosophical Association (Eastern Division); analyzes
the role and transformation of philosophy under the impact of the Great Proletarian Cultural Revolution.

Foreign Broadcast Information Service. Communist China:
Material on Cultural Revolution. 4 vols. Washington, D.C.:
Foreign Broadcast Information Service, May 24, June 5,
June 12, June 20, 1967. 60 + 79 + 90 + 74 pp.

These four supplements to Daily Report of the Foreign
Broadcast Information Service contain early documents
on the Great Proletarian Cultural Revolution taken mainly
from Chinese Communist radio broadcasts. Beginning
with Volume II, the material is presented by locality in
chronological order.

FRIEDMAN, Edward. "Cultural Limits of the Cultural

Revolution." Asian Survey, 9 (March 1969), 188-201.

Most studies of the Great Proletarian Cultural Revolution are absorbed with the ups and downs of China's political elite. Friedman examines some of the larger changes in social relations and tensions which produced these unforeseen responses and which continued to limit drastically the possibilities open to China's leaders.

GAYN, Mark. "Mao's Last Revolution." The 1968 World Book Year Book. Chicago: Field Enterprises Educational Corporation, 1968.

A picture of Mao's life and his political struggle during the Great Proletarian Cultural Revolution.

GITTINGS, John. "The Anti-Liu Shao-ch'i Campaign: the Crimes of China's K." Far Eastern Economic Review, 60 (April 18, 1968), 176-179.

Analyzes the charges against Liu in the field of foreign policy.

————. "China's Anti-Rightist Campaign: Stamping on the Rightists." Far Eastern Economic Review, 60 (May 2, 1968), 253-259.

An examination of the anti-Rightist campaign in the light of the dismissal at the end of March 1968 of the PLA chief of staff, Yang Cheng-wu, and a look at the basic issues behind these developments.

————. "Chinese Communist Party: The Millers' Tale." Far Eastern Economic Review, 65 (July 31, 1969), 283-286.

Study of the establishment of a Revolutionary Committee at Shanghai No. 17 State Cotton Mill and its effect upon current Party policies.

————. "The Cultural Revolution: The State of the Party."

58

Far Eastern Economic Review, 59 (February 29, 1968), 375-380.

Argues that the Great Proletarian Cultural Revolution has always been in essence a movement for Party rectification, rather than a "struggle for power" or a dispute over particular questions of policy.

GOLDMAN, Merle. "The Aftermath of China's Cultural Revolution." *Current History*, 61 (September 1971), 165-170.

A brief discussion of the rebuilding of the political structure after the Great Proletarian Cultural Revolution, the economic aftermath, the educational program since the GPCR, and the outcomes of the GPCR.

————. "The Fall of Chou Yang." *The China Quarterly*, No. 27 (July-September 1966), 132-148.

GRAY, Jack, and Patrick Cavendish. *Chinese Communism in Crisis: Maoism and the Cultural Revolution*. New York: Frederick A. Praeger, 1968. 279 pp.

The authors trace the historical development of the Great Proletarian Cultural Revolution and show how it first began by attempting to rectify errors occurring in the popular cultural sphere, which worked through the educational structure, and ultimately reached the political hierarchy. The authors also examine the political role of the intelligentsia in the light of the intellectual movements in China since the beginning of the century. Twelve documentary appendices form approximately half of the book.

The Great Cultural Revolution in China. Compiled and edited by the Asia Research Center. Melbourne & Sydney: Paul Flesch and Co., 1968. 507 pp.

A compilation of documents tracing the origin and events of the Great Proletarian Cultural Revolution from 1963 to the latter part of 1966. Part I consists of two chapters devoted to the prelude of the GPCR. Part II, with six chapters, covers the GPCR to the end of 1966, including an annotated personnel directory of key officials involved in the first phase of the GPCR. All documents were selected from Chinese Communist newspapers, press releases, Party publications, speeches of political leaders, etc. The volume also contains a chronology of events covering the period from November 1965 to November 1966, a glossary of terms and slogans, and a list of Chinese Communist newspapers and periodicals.

The Great Power Struggle in China. Hong Kong: Asia Research Center, 1969. 503 pp.

A companion volume to The Great Cultural Revolution in China, this book is also a compilation of source materials from China on the latter phase of the Great Proletarian Cultural Revolution. Documents are arranged under nine headings: The Red Guard Movement; Spread of the Revolution to the Countryside and to Industrial and Mining Enterprises; January Revolution; Nationwide Struggle to Seize Power; Reverse in the Power Struggle; the Impact of the Power Struggle; the Army's New Role in Cultural Revolution; the Cultural Revolution in the Army; and Problems Involving the Army. A portion of the Appendix is the same as that to be found in the previous volume.

The Great Socialist Cultural Revolution in China. 10 vols. Peking: Foreign Languages Press, 1966-67.

Volume 1 to 7 are under the title cited above, Volume 8 to 10 are under the new title, The Great Proletarian Cultural Revolution in China. This set is an official collection of important editorials of major newspapers; speeches and articles by leaders of the GPCR; messages, telegrams, notices from central and local revolutionary groups.

60

Great Victory for Chairman Mao's Revolutionary Line.
Peking: Foreign Languages Press, 1967. 88 pp.

A collection of speeches by Chou En-lai, Chiang Ch'ing,
Hsieh Fu-chih, and Chang Chun-chiao and editorials of
Jen-min jih-pao [People's Daily], and Chieh-fang-chün
pao [Liberation Army Daily] on the birth of the Peking
Municipal Revolutionary Committee, April 20, 1967.

GUNAWARDHANA, Theja. China's Cultural Revolution. Colombo, Ceylon: Colombo Apothecaries' Co., 1967. 264 pp.

A Sinhalese analysis of the Great Proletarian Cultural
Revolution; Chapter VIII is on "Universities and the Cultural Revolution" (pp. 83-92).

HARMAN, Richard Snyder. "The Maoist Case Against Liu
Shao-ch'i (1967): A Leadership Crisis in the Chinese
People's Republic." Unpublished Ph.D. dissertation, Uni-
versity of Virginia, 1969. 300 pp.

Mao Tse-tung and Liu Shao-ch'i were regarded as the
closest of political friends. This author argues that the
central contentions in the Maoist case suggested that Liu
and Mao were basically in opposition all along and that
Liu's line was essentially a revisionist line in contrast
to that of Mao.

HSIAO, Gene T. "The Background and Development of 'The
Proletarian Cultural Revolution.'" Asian Survey, 7
(June 1967), 389-404.

Discussion of the background and development of the Great
Proletarian Cultural Revolution under the following subjects: de-Stalinization and its impact on Mao and the CCP;
the Hundred Flowers movement and the antirightist campaign; the commune system and Mao's abdication as the
head of state, the fifth rectification and Mao's "flight" to
Shanghai; the beginning of an open power struggle; the

61

development of the power struggle. It concludes that "Mao
is in control of the situation and may eventually win the
struggle with the continued support of the majority of the
PLA."

HSIUNG, V. T. Red China's Cultural Revolution. New York:
Vantage Press, 1968. 188 pp.

Commences with the birth of communism in China in 1917
and sketches the infiltration into, and struggles with, the
Kuomintang during World War II. The author then analyzes
the progress of the ideological subtleties and the complex-
ities of Mao Tse-tung's thought. The author discusses individuals and factions, the Red Guard, the split in the international Communist Movement and offers his predictions
for the future.

HSU, Kai-yu. "The Chinese Communist Leadership." Current
History, 57 (September 1969), 129-134.

Discusses the struggles among the Communist leaders,
especially during the Great Proletarian Cultural Revolution, and analyzes the realigned leadership of the CCP
rebuilt at the Ninth Congress.

Hung-ch'i [Red Flag]. "Confessions Concerning the Line of
Soviet-U.S. Collaboration Pursued by the New Leaders of
the CPSU." No. 2 (1966). Translated in Selections from
China Mainland Magazines, No. 514 (March 7, 1966).

A severe attack on the new leaders who follow Khrushchev's revisionist line.

HUNG, Yu-chiao. The Effect of the "Cultural Revolution" on
the Chinese Communists' Economy. Taipei: Asian People's
Anti-Communist League, 1969. 62 pp.

Includes a review of the disbanding of financial and economic leadership organizations and the chaotic situation

62

of agricultural production in 1967. It then discusses the serious damage to industrial production, the anarchic state of commercial enterprises, and the decline in foreign trade. It concludes with a prediction of the probable course of economic development under Mao's direction.

I, Fan. Wen-ke hsia ti Chung-kung ching-chi [Communist Chinese Economy Under the Cultural Revolution]. Hong Kong: Union Research Institute, 1969. 250 pp.

Jen-min jih-pao [People's Daily]. "New Victory for Mao Tse-tung's Thought." June 4, 1966. Translated in Survey of China Mainland Press, No. 3714 (June 8, 1966), 12-13.

This editorial was written immediately after the Party's Peking Municipal Committee was reorganized and President Lu P'ing of Peking University was dismissed.

————. "Tear Aside the Bourgeois Mask of 'Liberty, Equality and Fraternity.'" June 4, 1966. Translated in Survey of China Mainland Press, No. 3714, (June 8, 1966), 1-8.

Bourgeois authorities, including Party intellectuals, were attacked for their reactionary world outlook — liberty, equality, and fraternity. Mao's thought was not to be challenged by any other ideology.

JOFFE, Ellis, "China in Mid-1966: 'Cultural Revolution' or Struggle for Power?" The China Quarterly, No. 27 (July-September 1966), 123-131.

JOHNSON, Chalmers. "China: The Cultural Revolution in Structural Perspective." Asian Survey, 8 (January 1968), 1-15.

JONES, P. H. M. "The Cultural Revolution: The Fights Among the Factions." Far Eastern Economic Review, 59 (February 1, 1968), 187-189.

Describes the spate of reports of new clashes in many

63

provinces, and speculation whether the army can contain the situation.

KAWAZOE, Noborn. Chugoku no bunka daikakumei [The Great Cultural Revolution in China]. Tokyo: Aoki Shoten, 1968. 228 pp.

KITTS, Charles. "The Great Proletarian Cultural Revolution." Issues & Studies, 6 (August 1970) 29-35.

Focuses on the domestic political situation whereby the author tries to answer the following questions about the Cultural Revolution: Why did it occur? When? What took place? Was it successful? If so, for whom? If not, why not? What were the results? What is the future of China?

KLEIN, Donald W. "Victims of the Great Proletarian Cultural Revolution." The China Quarterly, No. 27 (July-September 1966), 162-165.

Political biographies of P'eng Chen and Lu Ting-i.

Kuang-ming jih-pao [Kuangming Daily]. "Chronology of Wu Han's Anti-Communist, Anti-People, Counter-Revolutionary Activities in the Forties." May 6, 1966. Translated in Survey of China Mainland Press, No. 3709 (June 1, 1966), 10-27.

A chronology of activities and writings of Wu Han between 1940 and 1949.

KUNG, Teh-liang. "Developments of the Chinese Communist 'Great Cultural Revolution.'" Issues & Studies, 3 (January 1967), 20-27.

Discusses "criticism by name," obstructed production, "exchanging revolutionary experience on foot," and internal conflicts caused by the Red Guards.

Kung-fei li-tz'u wen-i cheng-feng chen-hsiang [The Chinese

64

Communists' Successive Rectifications in Literary and Art Fields]. Taipei: The Sixth Division of the Kuomintang Central Committee, 1970. 365 pp.

Except for the first chapter, which is an introduction on the development of Leftist literature in China and the first four Communist literary rectification campaigns, deals exclusively with the latest rectification activities during the Great Proletarian Cultural Revolution. In addition to the fields of literature and art, the book also devotes sections to journalism, education, and science. It provides a description of the leading figures purged and of the works denounced. A table of all persons in each field known to have been rectified and the reasons for their rectification is included.

KUO, Heng-yu. Maos Kulturrevolution; Analyse einer Karikatur. Pfullingen: Neske, 1968. 92 pp.

LEVENSON, Joseph R. "Communist China in Time and Space: Roots and Restlessness." The China Quarterly, No. 34 (July-September 1969), 1-11.

LI, Tien-min. "The People's Commune: Focal Point of Resistance to the Cultural Revolution." Issues & Studies, 6 (October 1969), 43-52.

Discusses the Great Proletarian Cultural Revolution in rural areas since the issuance of the "Instruction on the Cultural Revolution in Rural Areas (Draft)" by the CCP Central Committee on November 17, 1967, to the "power-seizure struggle" and attacks of Liu Shao-ch'i, and the situation of the communes in the early part of 1969.

Literaturnaya gazeta. "USSR's Literary Gazette Reviews Mao's Cultural Revolution." 24 (June 14, 1967). Translated in Joint Publications Research Service, No. 41735, Regular Series (July 7, 1967).

MA, Sitson. "We Are Slaves Who Have Been Betrayed." Life,

63 (July 14, 1967), 64-66, 69-73.

The musician who escaped from the Red Guards describes the destruction of Chinese intellectuals under Mao Tse-tung.

MA, Smarlo. "The Aftermath of Communist China's Cultural Revolution." Hong Kong: Chih Luen Press, 1971. 4 pp.

A paper read on January 12, 1971, at the 28th International Congress of Orientalists, Canberra, Australia, analyzing the cultural and educational situation in China after the Great Proletarian Cultural Revolution.

MARCHAIS, Albert. Revolution culturelle et expression artistique. Paris: Centre d'Etudes Socialistes, 1967. 36 pp.

MILLER, A. C. "Impact of the Cultural Revolution." Atlantic Monthly, 222 (August 1968), 14-17.

MYRDAL, Jan, and Gun Kessle. China: The Revolution Continued. Translated from the revised Swedish edition by Paul Britten Austin. New York: Pantheon Books, 1970. 201 pp.

The authors interviewed the villagers of Liu Ling in northern Shensi Province and reported on the nature of the Great Proletarian Cultural Revolution at the village level and its effect on the structure of local government, finance and investment, the roles of various groups within the community, and women's liberation.

NEUHAUSER, Charles. "The Impact of the Cultural Revolution on the Chinese Communist Party Machine." Asian Survey, 8 (June 1968), 465-488.

New China News Agency. "A Great Revolution That Touches the People to Their Very Souls." June 2, 1966. Reprinted in Survey of China Mainland Press, No. 3713 (June 7, 1966), 1-3.

English text of an editorial in Jen-min jih-pao [People's

66

Daily] emphasizes the existence of contradictions and class struggle on the ideological and cultural front and warns that the Hungarian incident was started by a number of revisionist writers of the Petofi Club.

―――. "Never Forget Class Struggle." May 4, 1966. Translated in Survey of China Mainland Press, No. 3696 (May 12, 1966), 5-10.

An editorial of Chieh-fang-chün pao [Liberation Army Daily] attacks certain "anti-Party, antisocialist elements" and warns members of the Peoples Liberation Army against "unarmed enemies."

―――. "Tear Aside the Bourgeois Mask of 'Liberty, Equality and Fraternity.'" June 4, 1966. Reprinted in Survey of China Mainland Press, No. 3714 (June 8, 1966), 1-8.

An editorial of Jen-min jih-pao [People's Daily] attacks the "bourgeois" world outlook and warns that anyone who opposes the Party, socialism, the proletarian dictatorship, and the thought of Mao Tse-tung must be overthrown, no matter how high his post may be.

NOUMOFF, S. J. "China's Cultural Revolution as a Rectification Movement." Pacific Affairs, 40 (Fall-Winter 1967-1968), 221-234.

OKSENBERG, Michel C., Carl Riskin, Robert A. Scalapino, and Ezra F. Vogel. The Cultural Revolution: 1967 in Review. With an Introduction by Alexander Eckstein. Ann Arbor: Center for Chinese Studies, University of Michigan, 1968. 125 pp.

This monograph consists of four papers prepared originally for a research conference convened by the University of Michigan Center for Chinese Studies in March 1968. They are: "Occupational Groups in Chinese Society and the Cultural Revolution," by Michel Oksenberg; "The Chinese Economy in 1967," by Carl Riskin; "The Cultural

Revolution and Chinese Foreign Policy," by Robert A. Scalapino; "The Structure of Conflict: China in 1967," by Ezra F. Vogel.

PENG, Shu-tse, Pierre Frank, Joseph Hansen, and George Novack. Behind China's "Great Cultural Revolution." New York: Merit Publishers, 1967. 63 pp.

Contains four articles and an introduction: "Peng Shu-tse on Background of Chinese Events;" "Second Interview with Peng Shu-tse: Mao's 'Cultural Revolution' "; "Meaning of the Shanghai Events," by Pierre Frank; "The Upheaval in China, an Analysis of the Contending Forces," by George Novack and Joseph Hansen. All articles were published previously between August 1966 and February 1967.

PINCHERELE, Alberto. La Revolution culturelle de Mao. Traduit de l'italien par Jean-Louis Faivre d'Arcier. Paris: Flammarion, 1968. 221 pp.

————. La rivoluzione culturale in Cina, ovvero Il convitato di pietra. Milano: Bompiani, 1967. 197 pp.

POSSONY, Stefan T. The Revolution of Madness. Taipei: Institute of International Relations, 1971.

Divided into two parts: "Brainwashing and Thought Reform" and "Cultural Revolution." The first part, under the title "The Revolution of Madness," is included in the Collected Documents of the First Sino-American Conference on Mainland China, published by the same institute, 1971.

POWELL, Ralph L. "The Power of the Chinese Military." Current History, 59 (September 1970), 129-133.

The author analyzes the military activities in the political field and the military support in the power struggle. Included in his study is a discussion of the role that the military have played in education during the Great Proletarian

68

Cultural Revolution.

Pravda. "Pravda Editorial on Chinese Imperialism, 1970."
Current History, 59 (September 1970), 173-174.

An English version of an editorial of Pravda, the Soviet
Communist Party newspaper, distributed by Tass on
May 18, 1970, attacking the Chinese Communist leaders,
including a paragraph on the suspension of schools during
the Great Proletarian Cultural Revolution.

Problems of Communism. "More on Maoism." 16 (March-
April 1967), 91-99.

A symposium on Maoism under the title "What Is Maoism?"
was initiated in the September-October 1966 issue of this
periodical. The discussion is continued here with I-kua
Chou's commentary, "The Mind of a Revolutionary," which
focuses primarily on the ideological derivations of Maoist
doctrine and the relative importance of nationalism and
Communist ideology in Mao's thinking and policies. This
is followed by a further, and final, exchange between
Stuart R. Schram and Arthur A. Cohen growing out of the
latter's concluding remarks to the original symposium.

―――. "The New Revolution." 15 (November-December
1966), 2-27.

Contains three articles. Harry Gelman in his article
"Mao and the Permanent Purge" attempts to clarify such
questions as: What was the genesis of the Great Proletarian Cultural Revolution and the far-reaching political
purge that evolved from it during 1966? What inspired
the rise of inner-Party opposition to Mao, and who were
the personalities involved? What have been the respective
roles of Mao, of Liu Shao-ch'i, of Lin Piao? In the article
"A Nation in Agony," Theodore Hsi-en Chen analyzes the
broader significance of the GPCR in the framework of the
Communist effort to remold "the minds and hearts" of the

Chinese people. Michael Freeberne, in "The Great Splash Forward," looks at the bemusing episode of Mao's spectacular swim in the Yangtze in July 1965 and the way it has been used to propagate the "cult of Mao."

————. "The New Revolution: II." 16 (March-April 1967), 1-10.

In the earlier series, Harry Gelman and Theodore Hsi-en Chen viewed the Great Proletarian Cultural Revolution as revolving primarily around internal issues. In this second series, Ross Terrill, in "The Siege Mentality," presents a different interpretation which sees the genesis of the GPCR above all in Communist China's "siege mentality" and growing fear of "U.S. imperialist aggression."

————. "The New Revolution: III." 16 (May-June 1967), 1-21.

The third section of the series contains two articles. In "Ideology Redivivus," Richard D. Baum's analysis pictures the Great Proletarian Cultural Revolution as part of a broader movement of "ideological revivalism" representing the Maoist leadership's answer to the dilemma of a revolutionary ideology already beginning to decrease under the impact of modernization. Franz Michael, in "The Struggle for Power," sees the current disturbance in China as the climax of a losing, two-sided struggle by Mao to impose his radical, utopian brand of communism at home and assert his claim to world Communist leadership abroad.

————. "The New Revolution: IV." 17 (March-April 1968), 1-30.

This last section of the series contains three articles. In "The Economic Cost," Jan Prybyla examines whether Communist China's economy has really suffered from the Great Proletarian Cultural Revolution and how its long-range goals of economic development and modernization have been affected. Victor C. Funnell, in his article "Social stratification," focuses attention on the process of

70

social stratification in China (PRC), seeing in Mao's determination to reverse it and restore old Marxist egalitarianism one of the key motivating factors of the GPCR. In "Mao and Stalin's Mantle," David E. Powell compares Mao's ideological rationale for the GPCR with some of the theories used by Stalin to justify the "Great Purge" of the 1930s and the "vigilance campaign" of the late 1940s and early 1950s.

————. "What Is Maoism? A Symposium." 15 (September-October 1966), 1-30.

The "Thought of Mao Tse-tung" became the only ideological guideline during the Great Proletarian Cultural Revolution. In this symposium, Stuart R. Schram's "The Man and His Doctrines" and Arthur A. Cohen's "The Man and His Politics" both discuss with different approaches, five specific aspects: (1) the key operational factors in Mao's political thought; (2) Mao's view of the role of intellectuals in a "socialist" society; (3) Mao's political "style" as reflected in his leadership of the Chinese Communist Party; (4) the practical significance of Mao's approach to international relations, especially with regard to "liberation war"; (5) the relative weight of Chinese and Marxist-Leninist components in shaping Mao's motives, thought, and personality. The symposium concludes with commentaries from other specialists.

PRYBLA, Jan S. "The Soviet View of Mao's Cultural Revolution." Virginia Quarterly Review, 44 (Summer 1968), 385-398.

PUSEY, James R. Wu Han: Attacking the Present Through the Past. Cambridge, Mass.: East Asian Research Center, Harvard University, 1969. 84 pp.

An analysis of the motivations and means employed in the Wu Han case of "protest through literature."

RAO, C. R. M. "The Uncertain Revolution." China Report, 4 (January-February 1968), 1-4.

ROBINSON, Joan. The Cultural Revolution in China. Baltimore: Penguin Books, 1969. 151 pp.

Divided into five parts: 1. Introduction; 2. The Cultural Revolution Seen from Shanghai; 3. Documents; 4. Reports and Conversations; and 5. Postscript. The centerpiece of this volume is part 2: The Cultural Revolution Seen from Shanghai. This account of the Cultural Revolution was given to Joan Robinson "in November, 1967, by a member of the committee then forming the 'temporary organ of power' in control of the municipality of Shanghai." The article "Cultural Revolution in China," which was incorporated in this book, appeared in International Affairs, 44 (April 1968), 214-227.

ROBINSON, Thomas W. "Chou En-lai's Role in China's Cultural Revolution." Santa Monica, Calif.: The Rand Corporation, 1969. IV, 194 pp.

————, Richard Baum, William F. Dorrill, Melvin Gurtov, and Harry Harding, Jr. The Cultural Revolution in China. Berkeley: University of California Press, 1971. 600 pp.

Offers five case studies on central features of the Great Proletarian Cultural Revolution by as many authors. The authors assess the political and ideological background of the Cultural Revolution, provide detailed accounts of some aspects of its political history, and discuss its effect on Chinese foreign policy.

RUSSELL, Maud. The Ongoing Cultural Revolution in China. New York: Maud Russell, Publisher (n.d.). 28 pp.

A special issue of Far East Reporter. Based primarily on secondary sources, it reports briefly on some aspects

72

of the ongoing Cultural Revolution during 1968, with a
short section on "A New Educational System."

—————. Some Background on China's Great Proletarian Cultural Revolution. New York: Maud Russell, Publisher
(n.d.). 40 pp.

A special issue of Far East Reporter. Based primarily
on secondary sources, it reports briefly on the Great Proletarian Cultural Revolution in 1966.

SARGENT, Margie, Vivienne B. Shue, Thomas J. Mathews,
and Deborah S. Davis. The Cultural Revolution in the
Provinces. Cambridge, Mass.: Harvard University
Press, 1971.

The four essays in this volume examine the Great Proletarian Cultural Revolution in four crucial localities —
Heilungkiang, Szechwan, Shanghai, and Wuhan — tracing
the outlines of the transformation of the original concep-
tions of the movement through a highly complex struggle
for prestige, political position, and ideological purity.

SCHELOCHOWZEW, S. Mao-kung wen-hua ta-ke-ming mu-chi
chi [Eyewitness Account of the Chinese Cultural Revo-
lution]. A Chinese translation of Chinesisch Kulturrevolution aus der Nahe. Translated by the Translation Bureau,
Ministry of Defense, Republic of China. Taipei: Ministry
of National Defense, 1970.

The author was a Soviet graduate student who studied
Chinese literature in Peking in 1966 and thus witnessed
the early phases of the Great Proletarian Cultural Revolution. After leaving China, he revised his diary of the
eight months, from February to October 1966, transforming it into a book for publication in West Germany by
Deutsche Verlagen in 1969. This book is based on his
own observations and information gathered from wall

posters as well as through his friends and teachers. As a student in Peking Normal University, he was particularly sensitive to the cultural aspects of the GPCR and the feelings of intellectuals.

SCHWARTZ, Benjamin I. "The Reign of Virtue: Some Broad Perspectives on Leader and Party in the Cultural Revolution." The China Quarterly, 35 (July-September 1968), 1-17.

SEYBOLT, Peter J. "China's Revolution in Education — The Struggle Between Two Lines." Canadian and International Education, No. 1 (June 1972), 29-41.

————. "The Yenan Revolution in Mass Education." The China Quarterly, No. 48 (October-December 1971), 641-669.

This article indicates the origins of many educational policies implemented during the Cultural Revolution, and concludes by comparing early revolutionary policies (1937-1945) with Cultural Revolution policies.

SNOW, Edgar. "Aftermath of the Cultural Revolution." New Republic, 164 (April 10, 1971), 18-21.

SOLAJIC, Dragutin. Kineska kulturna revolucija. Naslovna Strana: Pavle Ristic. Beograd, "Sedma sila," 1966. 63 pp.

SPITZ, R. "Mao's Permanent Revolution." Review of Politics, 30 (October 1968), 440-454.

Summary of the Forum on the Work in Literature and Art in the Armed Forces with Which Comrade Lin Piao Entrusted Comrade Chiang Ching. Peking: Foreign Languages Press, 1968. 48 pp.

Contents include "Comrade Lin Piao's Letter to Members of the Standing Committee of the Military Commission of the Party Central Committee (March 22, 1966)"; "Summary of the Forum on the Work in Literature and Art in the Armed Forces with Which Comrade Lin Piao Entrusted Comrade Chiang Ching"; "Two Diametrically Opposed Documents" (editorial of Hung-ch'i [Red Flag], No. 9, 1967); "An Important Document for the Proletarian Cultural Revolution" (editorial of Jen-min jih-pao [People's Daily], May 29, 1967); "Pick Up Your Pens and Hold on to Your Guns, Fight to Defend Proletarian State Power" (editorial of Chieh-fang-chün pao [Liberation Army Daily], May 29, 1967).

TING, Wang. "Plots and Counterplots." Far Eastern Economic Review, 59 (June 25, 1968), 147-152.

―――. "Power Struggle in Peking: Plots and Counterplots." Far Eastern Economic Review, 59 (January 25, 1968), 147-152.

Analysis of the situation of the vast upheavals in the political hierarchy of China during the Great Proletarian Cultural Revolution and discussion of the rise and fall of K'ang Sheng's career, pointing out that ever since his days as a master spy K'ang Sheng has shown a remarkable talent for survival.

―――. "Yao Wen-yuan: Newcomer in China's Politburo." Current Scene, 7 (July 15, 1969), 1-24.

Analysis of the family background of Yao and his activities during the earlier rectification campaigns, with special attention to the role that Yao played during the Great Proletarian Cultural Revolution and his rise to the political stage. Selections from Yao Wen-yüan's major articles published from 1965 to 1968 are appended.

UHALLEY, Stephen, Jr. "The Cultural Revolution and the Attack on the 'Three-Family Village.'" The China Quarterly, No. 27 (July-September 1966), 149-161.

75

An account of the cultural rectification campaign against Wu Han, Teng T'o, and Liao Mo-sha and its expansion to include Lu-P'ing, Kuang Hua-ming and, finally, the reorganization of the Peking Municipal Party Committee and the Peking University Party organ.

Union Research Service. "Liu Shao-ch'i's 'Self-Criticism.'" 51 (May 3, 1968), 117-128.

Two speeches in the style of "self-examination and self-criticism" of Liu Shao-ch'i made in October 1966, and sometime between April and July 1967, respectively.

————. "The Teng T'o Affair." 43 (June 3, 1966), 280-293.

Translation of four articles from Ta-kung pao, Peking, from May 12 to May 15, 1966, attacking Teng T'o and his associates.

VINACKE, Harold M. "The Continuing Chinese Revolution." Current History, 53 (September 1967), 161-166.

WANG, Hsüeh-wen. "The Nature and Development of the 'Great Cultural Revolution.'" Issues & Studies, 4 (September 1968), 11-21.

WATSON, Andrew. "Of Freaks and Monsters." Far Eastern Economic Review, 57 (August 24, 1967), 373-376.

WILSON, Dick. "The Cultural Revolution: The China After Next." Far Eastern Economic Review, 59 (February 1968), 189-195.

Examines the "platform" of the "opposition" in China — the political and economic policies which the adherents of Liu Shao-ch'i and others who are resisting Maoism are defending.

WU, Chi-fang. "The Impact of the 'Great Cultural Revolution'

76

on the Peiping Regime." Chinese Communist Affairs,
5 (August 1968), 41-59.

WU, Han. "On Hai Jui." Teng-hsia chi [Lamplight Collection].
Peking: San-lien Bookstore, 1961. Translated in Chinese
Studies in History and Philosophy, 1 (Winter 1968-69), 3-44.

A glimpse of Wu Han, the historian's, general interpretation of Hai Jui.

WU, Yuan-li. "Economics, Ideology and the Cultural Revolution." Asian Survey, 8 (March 1968), 223-235.

YAHUDA, Michael B. "China's Military Capabilities."
Current History, 57 (September 1969), 142-149, 182.

Includes a discussion of the functions of the People's
Liberation Army and the civic roles that they have played
during the Great Proletarian Cultural Revolution.

YAO, Wen-yüan. The Working Class Must Exercise Leadership
in Everything. Peking: Foreign Languages Press, 1968.
21 pp. Originally appeared in Hung-ch'i [Red Flag],
No. 2 (1968). Also translated in Selections from China
Mainland Magazines, No. 625 (September 3, 1968), 1-5.

Written when workers' Mao Tse-tung thought propaganda
teams entered both institutions of higher learning and
secondary schools, this article reveals the serious disintegration then existing as a result of the Great Proletarian
Cultural Revolution; it is one of the most important articles
written by Yao, member of the Cultural Revolution Group
under the Party Central Committee.

YU, Chiang-chiang. "How Teng T'o Shields Wu Han." Jen-min
jih-pao [People's Daily], May 14, 1966. Translated in
Survey of China Mainland Press, No. 3707 (May 27, 1966).

Teng T'o, formerly chief editor of Jen-min jih-pao, was said to have defended Wu Han, the playwright of Hai Jui's Dismissal from Office, in a forum held by Pei-ching jih-pao [Peking Daily], organ of the CCP Peking Municipal Committee, headed by the mayor, P'eng Chen.

ZANEGIN, B., A. Mironov, and Ya. Mikhaylov. "China and Its Cultural Revolution: A Soviet Analysis." (Originally published under the title: K Sobytiyam v Kitaye [On Events in China], by the Publishing House of Political Literature, USSR, 1967). Translated in Joint Publications Research Service, No. 48239 (June 16, 1969).

Examines the basic processes occuring in the area of economics and in the domestic and foreign policy of Communist China and tries to clarify the sources of the current policy of Mao Tse-tung and his group as well as the causes, content, and goals of the Great Proletarian Cultural Revolution.

ZHELOKHOVTSEV, A. La Revolution culturelle vue par un sovietique. Traduit du russe par Mme Slodzian et Jacques Michel. Paris: R. Laffont, 1968. 240 pp.

See also:

Asia. "Mainland China in the 1970's." 18 (Spring 1970), 16-36. [II]

CCP Documents of the Great Proletarian Cultural Revolution, 1966-1967. Hong Kong: Union Research Institute, 1968. 692 pp. [I]

The Case of P'eng Teh-huai, 1959-1968. Hong Kong: Union Research Institute, 1968. 515 pp. [I]

CHAI, Winberg, ed. Essential Works of Chinese Communism.

78

New York: Pica Press, 1970. 464 pp. [II]

China News Analysis. "Policy or Rivalry? The Roots of the
Cultural Revolution: The 1959 Lushan Meeting." No. 685
(November 17, 1967), 1-7. [II]

CHUNG, Hua-min, and Arthur C. Miller. Madame Mao — A
Profile of Chiang Ch'ing. Hong Kong: Union Research
Institute, 1968. 320 pp. [II]

Communist China, 1966. 2 vols. Hong Kong: Union Research
Institute, 1968. 251 + 282 pp. [I]

Communist China, 1967. 2 vols. Hong Kong: Union Research
Institute, 1969. 329 + 266 pp. [I]

Communist China, 1968. Hong Kong: Union Research Institute,
1969. 499 pp. [I]

Current Background. "Collection of Documents Concerning
the Great Proletarian Cultural Revolution." No. 852
(May 6, 1968), 1-136. [I]

———. "The Press Campaign Against Wu Han." No. 783
(March 21, 1966), 1-63. [I]

———. "Teng T'o, His 'Evening Talks at Yenshan' and the
'Three-Family Village' Group." No. 792 (June 29, 1966),
1-73. [I]

FAN, K. H., ed. The Chinese Cultural Revolution: Selected
Documents. New York: Grove Press, 1968. 320 pp. [I]

Far Eastern Economic Review. "China 1968: Sketches from
the Cultural Revolution." 62 (October 3, 1968), 74-75. [I]

GRAY, Jack, ed. Modern China's Search for a Political Form.

79

New York: Oxford University Press, 1969. 379 pp. [II]

HO, Ping-ti, and Tang Tsou, eds. China in Crisis. 2 vols. in 3. With a Forward by Charles U. Daly. Chicago: University of Chicago Press, 1968. 803 + 484 pp. [II]

HUANG, Chen-hsia. Chung-kung chun-jen chih [Chinese Communist Military Who's Who]. Hong Kong: Institute of Contemporary History, 1968. 823 pp. [I]

Index to Titles of English News Releases of Hsinhua News Agency, 1967. Hong Kong: Union Research Institute, 1968. 459 pp. [I]

KAO, Chung-yen. Chung-kung jen-shih pien-tung, 1959-1969 [Changes of Personnel in Communist China]. Hong Kong: Union Research Institute, 1970. 964 pp. [I]

LEWIS, John W. Party Leadership and Revolutionary Power in China. New York: Cambridge University Press, 1970. 422 pp. [II]

LI, Tien-min. Chou En-lai. Taipei: Institute of International Relations, 1970. 426 pp. [II]

LI, Ting-sheng. The CCP's Persecution of Chinese Intellectuals in 1949-69. Taipei: Asian People's Anti-Communist League, 1969. 67 pp. [II]

LIU, Shao-ch'i. Quotations from President Liu Shao-ch'i. With an Introduction by C. P. Fitzgerald. Melbourne: Paul Flesch, 1968. 223 pp. [I]

Long Live Victory of the Great Cultural Revolution Under the Dictatorship of the Proletariat. Peking: Foreign Languages Press, 1968. 49 pp. [I]

80

Min-kuo wu-shih-ch'i nien ti-ching ta-shih chi [Headline Events of the Chinese Communist Regime in 1968]. Taipei: Institute of Studies on Chinese Communist Affairs, National War College, 1969. 123 pp. [I]

NASHIMOTO, Yuhei. Chou En-lai. Tokyo: Keiso Shokyoku, 1967. [II]

1967 Fei-ch'ing nien-pao [1967 Yearbook on Chinese Communism]. Taipei: Institute for the Study of Chinese Communist Problems, 1967. 1958 pp. [I]

1968 Fei-ch'ing nien-pao [1968 Yearbook on Chinese Communism]. Taipei: Institute for the Study of Chinese Communist Problems, 1968. 1102 pp. [I]

1969 Chung-kung nien-pao [1969 Yearbook on Chinese Communism]. 2 vols. Taipei: Institute for the Study of Chinese Communist Problems, 1969. 1700 pp. [I]

Problems of Communism. "China in Flux." 18 (November-December 1969), 1-14. [II]

SCHICKEL, Joachim, ed. Mao Tse-tung: Der Grosse Strategische Plan. Dokumente zur Kulturrevolution. Berlin: Edition Voltaire, 1969. 583 pp. [XIV]

SPITZ, Allen A., ed. Contemporary China. Pullman, Washington: Washington State University, 1967. 56 pp. [II]

TENG, T'o. Yen-shan yeh-hua hsüan-chi [Selections from Evening Chats at Yenshan]. Hong Kong: Chih Luen Press, 1966. 157 pp. [I]

TING, Wang, ed. Pei-ching shih wen-hua ta-ke-ming yün-tung [The Great Cultural Revolution Movement in Peking City]. Hong Kong: Ming Pao Monthly, 1970. 688 pp. [I]

81

————, ed. P'eng Te-huai wen-ti chuan-chi [Special Collection on the Case of P'eng Te-huai]. Hong Kong: Ming Pao Monthly, 1969. 510 pp. [I]

————, ed. Teng T'o hsüan-chi [Selected Works of Teng T'o]. Hong Kong: Ming Pao Monthly, 1969. 582 pp. [I]

————, ed. Tou-cheng chung-yang chi-kuan tang-ch'üan p'ai [Struggle Against the Clique in Authority in Central Organizations]. Hong Kong: Ming Pao Monthly, 1967. 717 pp. [I]

————, ed. Wu Han yü "Hai Jui pa-kuan" shih-chien [Wu Han and the Affair of "Dismissal of Hai Jui"]. Hong Kong: Ming Pao Monthly, 1969. 750 pp. [I]

U.S. Department of State. Communist China. Washington, D.C.: U.S. Government Printing Office, 1969. 32 pp. [II]

VOGEL, Ezra F. Canton Under Communism: Programs and Politics in a Provincial Capital, 1949-1968. Cambridge, Mass.: Harvard University Press, 1969. 448 pp. [II]

WANG, Chang-ling. Chung-kung ti wen-i cheng-feng [Chinese Communist Rectification in Literature and Art Fields]. Taipei: Institute of International Relations, 1967. 264 pp. [II]

Who's Who in Communist China. 2 vols. Rev. ed. Hong Kong: Union Research Institute, 1969. 522 + 402 pp. [I]

WU, Chun-hsi. Dollars, Dependents and Dogma. Introduction by C. F. Remer. Stanford, Calif.: Hoover Institution on War, Revolution, and Peace, 1967. 237 pp. [II]

IV. General survey of education

BASTID, Marianne. "Economic Necessity and Political Ideals in Educational Reform During the Cultural Revolution." The China Quarterly, No. 42 (April-June 1970), 16-45.

Assesses the "respective weight of economic necessity and political ideals in educational reform in an attempt to shed some light on the nature of the new 'world outlook' which the Cultural Revolution advances. The analysis follows the dialectical process through which the new order is being worked out: that is, criticism of the old system, proposals for reform and the implementation of reform."

BOHLEN, Charles. "Education in China: Studies in Maoism." Far Eastern Economic Review, 67 (February 19, 1970), 19-22.

Discusses new educational policy, situation in the school system, problems of reopening schools, curriculum and textbooks, teachers and teaching methods after the educational reform, and the role that Mao Tse-tung Thought Propaganda Teams played.

BRATTON, Dale L. "Secondary Literature on Communist Chinese Education." Sociology of Education, 40 (Winter 1967), 80-89.

A review of some of the literature on education. A comparison with Soviet educational experience is developed and related to the Great Proletarian Cultural Revolution in Communist China. A selected bibliography of secondary literature is appended.

84

Centre d'Etude du Sud-Est Asiatique et de l'Extreme Orient. "Education in Communist China." 2 vols. Brussels, Belgium, February 18-19, 1969. (Mimeographed) 245 pp.

Includes 13 papers presented at the Fourth Working Session of the Centre. These are "Education in Traditional China (Period up to 1905)," by Tilemann Grimm; "Education in Pre-1949 China (Period 1905-1949)," by Wolfgang Franke; "Formal Organization of Education in Communist China," by Jürgen Domes; "Mass Education," by Marianne Bastid; "Teaching Methods, Examinations, Curricula, etc.," by Alexander Zubetz; "The Interruption of Higher Education and Its Ideological Justification," by Douwe W. Fokkema; "The Impact of the 'Hundred Flowers' Affair to the Cultural Revolution," by G. K. Kindermann; "Inner-Party Conflicts on Education and Youth Work in the Background of the Cultural Revolution," by W.A.C. Adie; "The Teaching of History in Communist China," by C.T. Hu; "Ideology and Education in Communist China," by Daniel Ellegiers; "Education and the Social Ideal in Communist China," by Cho-Yee To; "Les problemes economiques de l'enseignement chinois avant la revolution culturelle," by Michel Cartier. Each article is followed by a discussion.

Chiao-yü ke-ming [Educational Revolution]. "Chronology of the Two-Road Struggle on the Educational Front in the Past Seventeen Years." May 6, 1967. Translated in Chinese Education, 1 (Spring 1968), 3-58.

A chronology of the struggle on the education front between Mao's "proletarian educational line" and the "revisionist educational line" represented by Liu Shao-ch'i, in six periods: the period of rehabilitation and growth of people's education (1949-1952); the period of affirmation of socialist educational policy (1953-1957); the period of great educational revolution and development (1958-1960); the period of fluctuations of the educational revolution (1961-1963); the period of intensive development of struggle

85

between two lines and two command headquarters on the education front (1964-1965); the period of the Great Proletarian Cultural Revolution (1966-1967).

China Reconstructs. "Breaking Trails in the Revolution in Education." 19 (November 1970), 19-22.

CHU, Hung-ti. "Education in Mainland China." Current History, 59 (September 1970), 165-169.

The author analyzes the educational crisis during the Great Proletarian Cultural Revolution after a brief review of the traditional system, the modern school system, and ideological reform. He concludes that Mao's educational revolution "may be no more successful than the Great Leap Forward."

Current Scene. "China's Academic Reforms: A Progress Report." 9 (September 7, 1971), 20-22.

A short report on "curriculum reforms" and "change brings problems" after the reopening of Chinese schools.

HAWKINS, John N. Educational Theory in the People's Republic of China: The Report of Ch'ien Chun-jui. Honolulu: University of Hawaii Press, 1971. 120 pp. A revision of "The Theory and Practice of Education in the People's Republic of China." Unpublished M.A. dissertation, University of British Columbia, 1969. 180 pp.

A general study of education in China (PRC) which focuses on the effect of ideological campaigns on the practice of education; includes recent developments of the Great Proletarian Cultural Revolution and compares early Chinese educational theory (represented for the first time in English by a translation of one of the first important theoretical documents by former Vice Minister of Education Ch'ien Chun-jui) with post-Cultural Revolution statements.

86

HOOK, Brian. "Education Within Industry: China." Education
Within Industry. The World Year Book of Education, 1968.
New York: Harcourt, Brace & World, Inc., 1968.

A study of a segment of the composite education system
in China, namely that portion of the spare-time component
devoted to education within industry. The author discusses
its development in political, cultural, and economic aspects.

HU, Chang-tu, ed. Aspects of Chinese Education. New York:
Teachers College, Columbia University, 1969. 95 pp.

Contains five articles which appeared first in a special
issue of Comparative Education Review, February 1969,
entitled "Symposium on Aspects of Chinese Education."
The five chapters are: "Orthodoxy over Historicity: The
Teaching of History in Communist China," by C. T. Hu;
"Medical Education and Manpower in Communist China,"
by Leo A. Orleans; "The Language Issue in Communist
Chinese Education," by Susan Biele Alitto; "China's International, Cultural and Educational Relations: With Selected
Bibliography," by Stewart E. Fraser; and "The New Socialist Man," by Theodore Hsi-en Chen.

————. The Education of National Minorities in Communist
China. Washington, D.C.: U.S. Government Printing
Office, 1970. 30 pp. (OE-14146)

The author describes the education of some 54 national
minorities in China against the background of that country's domestic politics. The study shows how the regime's
attempts to integrate minority groups into the mainstream
of Chinese national life have affected its educational policies
in minority areas. The last section is devoted to the education of national minorities during the period of the Great
Proletarian Cultural Revolution.

KLEPIKOV, V. Z. "The Fate of Public Education in China."
Sovetskaia pedagogika, 8 (1968). Translated in Chinese

Education, 1 (Winter 1968), 37-49.

MACDOUGALL, Colina. "Education in China: Bringing Up
Baby." Far Eastern Economic Review, 63 (January 30,
1969), 194-195.

The author sees the decentralization of the Chinese education system as a move both to allow the government to
shed a heavy financial burden and to tighten up ideologically.

OLDHAM, C. H. G. "Technology in China: Science for the
Masses?" Far Eastern Economic Review, 60 (May 16,
1968), 353-355.

Outlines the violence of the struggle between the "two
lines" — the Maoists advocate a grass-roots emphasis
upon technology for the masses, the opposition favors
more attention to advanced research — and argues that
the future of Chinese science is inextricably linked to the
future of the Great Proletarian Cultural Revolution.

PRICE, R. F. Education in Communist China. London:
Routledge & Kegan Paul, 1970. 308 pp.

"The first section deals with policy and the important de-
bates going on; the next section analyses the major ob-
stacles to reform and the third section gives details of
schools, how they are organized, what kind of curricula
are provided, how they are financed, and how teachers
are trained" (Introduction). The final chapter is on "Students and the Cultural Revolution, 1966-1968."

SOLOMON, Richard H. "The Chinese Revolution and the
Politics of Dependency." Unpublished Ph.D. dissertation,
Massachusetts Institute of Technology, 1967. 464 pp.

"Chinese attitudes toward social authority, interpersonal
relations, and politics based on intensive interviews with
a sample of 89 Chinese of three generations are studied.

The objective is to look for the origins of adult political attitudes in childhood socialization experience both within the family and in school, and to see if early-acquired attitude and behavioral patterns are evident in adult attitudes and social and political life.... The second half relates popular social and political attitudes to problems of leadership and change in Chinese Communist revolution, primarily through an analysis of the writings of Mao Tse-tung."

TOWNSEND, James R. The Revolutionization of Chinese Youth: A Study of Chung-kuo Ch'ing-nien. Berkeley: Center for Chinese Studies, 1967. 71 pp.

TSANG, Chiu-sam. "Social Change in China — With Special Reference to Education." Seminar on Social Change in China, Centre of Asian Studies, University of Hong Kong, May 2, 1970. (Mimeographed) 15 pp.

The author discusses five stages of cultural and educational reform beginning with the first stage of 1942 to the fifth stage of the Great Proletarian Cultural Revolution and analyzes the principles of educational reform with some remarks on the GPCR.

———. Society, Schools & Progress in China. London: Pergamon Press, 1968. 333 pp.

Includes a survey of important determinants of social and educational policy: the historical background and the cultural heritage, the present political and administrative structure, including a short section discussing the impact of the Great Proletarian Cultural Revolution.

WHITEHEAD, Rhea Menzel. "How the Young Are Taught in Mao's China." Saturday Review, March 4, 1972, 40-45.

A description of education in China today. The author visited there in the summer of 1971.

See also:

ALITTO, Susan Biele. "The Language Issue in Communist Chinese Education." Comparative Education Review, 13 (February 1969), 43-59. [VII]

China Topics. "China's Education Problems." YB 427 (May 23, 1967). [I]

Collected Documents of the First Sino-American Conference on Mainland China. Taipei: Institute of International Relations, 1971. 951 pp. [I]

Current Background. "Revolution in Education." No. 846 (February 8, 1968), 1-56. [I]

FRASER, Stewart E., ed. Education and Communism in China: An Anthology of Commentary and Documents. London: Pall Mall Press, 1971. 614 pp. [I]

LEE, Hwa-wei. "The Recent Educational Reform in Communist China." School & Society, 96 (November 9, 1968), 395-400. [VIII]

MELBY, John F., ed. Contemporary China. Toronto: The Canadian Institute of International Affairs, 1968. 138 pp. [II]

REECE, Bob. "Education in China: More of the Same." Far Eastern Economic Review, 60 (June 13, 1968), 563-565. [VI]

SEYMOUR, James Dulles. "The Policies of the Chinese Communists Toward China's Intellectuals and Professionals." Unpublished Ph.D. dissertation, Columbia University, 1968. 318 pp. [XII]

V. Primary (elementary) education

Chung-kuo fu-nü [Women of China]. "Thrust Politics Forward, Train the Children to Become Successors of the Proletarian Revolutionary Cause [Editorial]." 6 (June 1, 1966), 40. Translated in Chinese Sociology and Anthropology, 1 (Fall 1968), 25-27.

HSI, Ch'i-hsiu. "Use the Class Viewpoint to Analyze Problems in the Education of Young Children." Chung-kuo fu-nü [Women of China], 11 (October 17, 1966), 22. Translated in Chinese Sociology and Anthropology, 1 (Fall, 1968), 35-38.

HSUAN, Wei-tung. "Put Mao Tse-tung's Thought in Command of Kindergarten Education." Kuang-ming jih-pao [Kuangming Daily], March 31, 1969. Translated in Survey of China Mainland Press, No. 4400 (April 23, 1969), 1-6.

Condemns the program for kindergarten education mapped out in 1960 by the former Department of Propaganda under the CCP Central Committee as the "black fruit of renegade, traitor, and scab Liu Shao-ch'i's counterrevolutionary revisionist line."

Hung-ch'i [Red Flag], "Persist in Running Schools with Diligence and Frugality to Serve Proletarian Politics — A Report on an Investigation in the Primary School Run by Yuch'ang Brigade. Chaoyuan Hsien, Heilungkiang Province, No. 6 (June 1, 1971). Translated in Selections from China Mainland Magazines, No. 707-708 (June 28-July 6, 1971),

92

59-66. Appears also in Chinese Education, V (Spring-Summer 1972), 96-109

"Introduces a rural primary school which advances in the orientation pointed out in the "May 7 Directive." This school adheres to the policy of self-reliance and hard struggle and runs itself with diligence and frugality. It persists in taking study as its main task and learning other things at the same time and has the poor and lower-middle peasants take part in its management. Citing living facts, the article shows educational revolution definitely can succeed if Chairman Mao's "May 7 Directive" is put into practice" (Editor, Hung-ch'i).

———. "A Primary School Run by the People Under the Control of the Poor and Lower-Middle Peasants." No. 5 (1968), 46-51. Translated in Chinese Education, 2 (Fall 1969), 28-36.

An investigative report from Liaoning Province concerning the experience of a primary school run by the people established by the Sung-shu Production Brigade of the Chien-yi Commune in Yingkow County.

———. "A Primary School Where Poor and Lower-Middle Peasants Hold Power." No. 5 (November 24, 1968). Translated in Selections from China Mainland Magazines, No. 638 (December 23, 1968), 15-19.

Another English translation of the investigative report from Liaoning Province.

Jen-min jih-pao [People's Daily]. "Primary and Middle School Operation in Urban Areas." December 2-27, 1968. Translated in Current Background, No. 870 (January 27, 1969), 1-43.

The entire issue contains selections from the various series on the operation of schools in cities and towns

93

originally published in Jen-min jih-pao from December 2 to December 27, 1968.

————. "The Red Sun Rises in the Hearts of the Red Young Fighters." March 11, 1968. Translated in Current Background, No. 845 (May 24, 1968), 25-26.

A primary school in Peking describes how the younger red fighters organized Mao Tse-tung's thought study classes and formed "red pairs."

New China News Agency. "An Example of Primary School Students in Studying the Thought of Mao Tse-tung." May 31, 1966. Translated in Survey of China Mainland Press, No. 3713 (June 7, 1966), 11-14.

Reports a visit to a children's group for the study of Mao's works in Chiangmen, Kwangtung. The group meets every Saturday evening to study Mao's works and diaries of Lei Feng, Wang Chieh, and other model characters.

————. "Primary, Secondary Schools Begin New School Year, Carry on Revolution." November 5, 1967. Translated in Survey of China Mainland Press, No. 4057 (November 8, 1967), 17-18.

Curriculum, teaching material, and teaching methods were all reformed in the schools in Peking and Shanghai. In addition, workers, peasants, and armymen were asked to deliver lectures and give pupils guidance.

P'AN, Lo-p'ei, and Kuan Tung-ping. "A Great Revolution in the Education of Children." Chung-kuo fu-nü [Women of China], 11 (October 17, 1966), 18-19. Translated in Chinese Sociology and Anthropology, 1 (Fall 1968), 28-34.

RIDLEY, Charles P., et al. The Making of a Model Citizen in Communist China. Stanford, Calif.: The Hoover Institution Press,

94

Stanford University, 1971. 404 pp.

Some 385 lessons taken from 10 volumes of elementary school textbooks (grades 1-5) are studied and analyzed. Of the total, 155 selections appear in translation at the end of this volume.

TSAI, Pei-hsun. "Use Material Dialectics to Handle the Relationship Between Character Reading and Teaching." Wen-tzu kai-ke [Written Language Reform], No. 3 (March 12, 1966). Translated in Selections from China Mainland Magazines, No. 529 (June 26, 1966), 32-35.

According to the author, "less but better" should be the principle of teaching language in primary schools. Intended to gather experience gained in teaching reform, some surveys had been conducted in a number of schools. It was disclosed that many first-graders had managed to learn only 50 percent of the 1,750 characters they were expected to know.

Union Research Service. "How Should Primary and Secondary Schools in Cities Be Run?" 54 (January 7, 1969), 15-30.

————. "Public Primary Schools to be 'Sent Down' to Rural Production Brigades." 53 (December 31, 1968), 353-369.

A collection of radio broadcasts and letters appearing in Jen-min jih-pao [People's Daily] (November 14, 1968) and Kuang-ming jih pao [Kuang-ming Daily] (November 19, 1968) on how poor and lower-middle peasants manage their schools.

See also:

FRASER, Stewart E. "Reforms for Rural Primary and Middle Schools." School & Society, 99 (April 1971), 237-241. [IX]

95

Jen-min jih-pao [People's Daily]. "'Education Program' Is Published in Good Time." May 19, 1969. Translated in Survey of China Mainland Press, No. 4429 (June 4, 1969), 9-10. [IX]

———. "Educational Program for Rural Middle and Primary Schools (Draft for Discussion)." May 12, 1969. Translated in Chinese Education, 2 (Winter 1969-70), 53-62. [IX]

———. "Forum on Entrusting Production Brigades to Run Primary Schools in the Countryside." (November 14-December 7, 1968). Translated in Current Background, No. 869 (January 15, 1969), 1-35. [IX]

———. "How Poor and Lower-Middle Peasants are Managing Schools." October 24, 1968. Translated in Chinese Education, 1 (Winter 1968-69), 6-12. [IX]

———. "Make It Convenient for Children of Poor and Lower-Middle Peasants to Go to School." May 19, 1969. Translated in Survey of China Mainland Press, No. 4429 (June 4, 1969), 13. [IX]

———. "Our Suggestions for Additions and Modifications to the Draft Education Program." May 19, 1969. Translated in Survey of China Mainland Press, No. 4429 (June 4, 1969), 14-15. [IX]

———. "Our Views and Suggested Modifications." May 26, 1969. Translated in Survey of China Mainland Press, No. 4438 (June 17, 1969), 9-10. [IX]

———. "Some Points of View Held by Us Poor and Lower-Middle Peasants." May 19, 1969. Translated in Survey of China Mainland Press, No. 4429 (June 4, 1969), 11-12. [IX]

Kuang-ming jih-pao [Kuang-ming Daily]. "Several Proposals

96

in Connection with the 'Program.' " May 24, 1969. Translated in Survey of China Mainland Press, No. 4440 (June 20, 1969), 6-7. [IX]

————. "With Cultural Power in Hand Peasants Should Compile Books." January 11, 1969. Translated in Survey of China Mainland Press, No. 4353 (February 5, 1969), 9-12. [IX]

New China News Agency. "Draft Program for Primary and Middle Schools in Chinese Countryside. May 13, 1969. Reprinted in Survey of China Mainland Press, No. 4418 (May 19, 1969), 9-15. [IX]

————. "Universities and Middle and Primary Schools Must Resume Classes While Making Revolution." October 24, 1967. Translated in Survey of China Mainland Press, No. 4049 (October 27, 1967), 1-3. [XIII]

VI. Secondary (middle) education

China Reconstructs. "Revolution in Education in a City Middle School" 18 (September 1969), 14-17.

> Reports the changes which occurred in the Lanchow No. 5 Middle School after the working class took over management and leadership.

FRASER, Stewart E. "High School: Chinese Communist Style." Class Mate (January 1967), 6-9.

> An account of some of the problems and successes encountered in providing middle and higher secondary education to millions of Chinese youth.

Hung-ch'i [Red Flag]. "A Factory Runs a School and the School Makes Two Links." No. 2 (1969), 30-35. Translated in Chinese Education, 2 (Winter 1969-70), 3-13.

> An investigative report of Lanchow City, Kansu Province, on a city secondary school being run by a factory.

————. "'May 7 Directive' Is the Guideline for Educational Revolution — Report on an Investigation of Hsin-i Middle School, Hsin-i Hsien, Kwangtung." No. 6 (June 1, 1971). Translated in Selections from China Mainland Magazines, No. 707-708 (June 28-July 6, 1971), 50-58. Appears also in Chinese Education, 5 (Spring-Summer 1972), 82-95.

> "Presents some experiences of a middle school in overall implementation of the "May 7 Directive." Applying

98

Chairman Mao's philosophical thinking, the school has come to recognize that "taking study as the main task and learning other things at the same time" is a complete policy, and has correctly handled the connection between "taking study as the main task" and "learning other things at the same time," the connection between the classroom in the school and the classroom in the society, and the connection between political movements and teaching work. In its teaching work, the school lays emphasis on enabling its students to comprehend deeply and master conscientiously book knowledge through practical work; in regard to practical experiences, it puts the emphasis on enabling the students to elevate their practical experience into theoretical knowledge through practice again" (Editor, Hung-ch'i).

Jen-min jih-pao [People's Daily]. "Hungch'i Middle School in Penhsi, Liaoning, Forms Textbook Compiling Group." May 8, 1969. Translated in Survey of China Mainland Press, No. 4419 (May 20, 1969), 6-7.

Suggests that the thought of Mao Tse-tung and politics should be emphasized in compiling new textbooks.

Kuang-ming jih-pao [Kuangming Daily]. "Advance Victoriously Along the Splendid Route Indicated by Chairman Mao." March 7, 1969. Translated in Survey of China Mainland Press, No. 4386 (March 28, 1969), 1-5.

Reports the reorganization of the Yenan Middle School of Tientsin. All children of workers and poor peasants of a suitable age in the vicinity are admitted to the school without examination.

————. "Bold Experiments in Pedagogic Reform." January 25, 1969. Translated in Survey of China Mainland Press, No. 4359 (February 13, 1969), 6-8.

Describes educational reforms carried out by workers of a silk factory of Feng-ch'eng, Liaoning Province, who took over the management of a middle school.

99

————. "Doing a Good Job in Operating Intermediate Technical Schools Is Essential to Socialist Construction." September 10, 1969. Translated in Survey of China Mainland Press, No. 4505 (September 29, 1969), 6-8.

The article admits that a shortage of trained technical personnel has already caused considerable losses to the country's economy.

————. "Resolutely Implement Chairman Mao's Directive on Resumption of Classes to Make Revolution." April 23, 1969. Translated in Survey of China Mainland Press, No. 4409 (May 6, 1969), 6-10.

Reports problems and resistance to the resumption of classes and making revolution in a middle school in Peking.

LI, Ts'ai. "My Views on How to Operate Intermediate Technical Schools Well." Kuang-ming jih-pao [Kuangming Daily]. September 10, 1969. Translated in Survey of China Mainland Press, No. 4505 (September 29, 1969), 9-11.

The author suggests: (1) leadership power over secondary technical schools must be in the hands of workers and poor and lower-middle peasants; (2) secondary technical schools and technicians schools can be combined and jointly run by factories and communes; (3) teachers for secondary technical schools should be drawn from workers and poor and lower-middle peasants.

New China News Agency. "Middle School Teaching Material Compiled Under Working Class Leadership." March 18, 1969. Reprinted in Survey of China Mainland Press, No. 4383 (March 25, 1969), 12-13.

————. "More Than 230 Middle Schools in Peking Have Brought About Revolutionary Great Alliance According to Class or Grade and Many Schools Have Resumed Classes to Make Revolution." October 22, 1967. Reprinted in Survey of China Mainland Press, No. 4051 (October 31, 1967).

100

————. "A Polytechnical School Welcomed by Poor and Lower-Middle Peasants." March 18, 1969. Reprinted in Survey of China Mainland Press, No. 4383 (March 25, 1969), 13-15.

————. "Revolutionary Teachers and Students of Shanghai K'ungchiang Middle School Conduct Revolutionary Mass Criticism and Repudiation on the One Hand and Explore Ways of Teaching Reform on the Other." October 24, 1967. Translated in Survey of China Mainland Press, No. 4057 (November 8, 1967), 11-14.

Reports that the teachers and students of K'ungchiang Middle School of Shanghai are now exploring ways of educational reform in accordance with Mao's "May 7" Directive.

Peking Review. "Urban Educational Revolution in Progress: A School Managed by Workers and Linked Up with a People's Commune and a PLA Unit." No. 7 (February 14, 1969), 3-7.

REECE, Bob. "Education in China: More of the Same." Far Eastern Economic Review, 60 (June 13, 1968), 563-565.

The author visited high schools in Peking and Changsha in 1968 and spoke to leaders, teachers, and students in these and other cities. His observations of classroom situations give an idea of events in some areas after resumption of classes.

Union Research Service. "Educational Reform Plan of Peking No. 23 Secondary Schools." 50 (January 12, 1968), 44-56.

Contains material concerning educational reform selected from the Red Guard tabloid "Steel August 1 Combat Flag" and "Educational Reform Bugle," a combined issue published jointly by the General Headquarters of Cultural, Educational, and Hygienic Systems of Mao Tse-tung's Thought, August 1 Combat Corps, and the Educational Revolution

101

Liaison Station of Canton District, December 1967.

See also:

FRASER, Stewart E. "Reforms for Rural Primary and Middle Schools." School & Society, 99 (April 1971), 237-241. [IX]

Hung-ch'i [Red Flag]. "A New Type of School That Combines Theory with Practice." No. 4 (1968), 24-31. Translated in Chinese Education, 2 (Fall 1969), 15-27. [I]

Jen-min jih-pao [People's Daily]. "Chairman Mao's 'March 7' Directive Is the Beacon Light Guiding Us Forward." March 12, 1968. Translated in Current Background, No. 854 (May 24, 1968), 27-33. [XIV]

————. "'Education Program' Is Published in Good Time." May 19, 1969. Translated in Survey of China Mainland Press, No. 4429 (June 4, 1969), 9-10. [IX]

————. "Educational Program for Rural Middle and Primary Schools (Draft for Discussion)." May 12, 1969. Translated in Chinese Education, 2 (Winter 1969-70), 53-62. [IX]

————. "Five Major Charges Against the Old Educational System." December 17, 1967. Translated in Survey of China Mainland Press, No. 4100 (January 16, 1968), 9-11. [X]

————. "'May 7' Agricultural Senior Middle School Set Up in Commune in Honan." April 21, 1969. Translated in Survey of China Mainland Press, No. 4408 (May 5, 1969), 1-4. [IX]

————. "Our Suggestions for Additions and Modifications to the Draft Education Program." May 19, 1969. Translated in Survey of China Mainland Press, No. 4429 (June 4, 1969), 14-15. [IX]

102

―――. "Our Views and Suggested Modifications." May 26, 1969. Translated in Survey of China Mainland Press, No. 4438 (June 17, 1969), 9-10. [IX]

―――. "Primary and Middle School Operation in Urban Areas." December 2-27, 1968. Translated in Current Background, No. 870 (January 27, 1969), 1-43. [V]

―――. "Proletarian Force of Teachers of a New Type Set Up in Shihchingshan Middle School, Peking." February 10, 1969. Translated in Survey of China Mainland Press, No. 4364 (February 26, 1969), 3-5. [VII]

―――. "Some Points of View Held by Us Poor and Lower-Middle Peasants." May 19, 1969. Translated in Survey of China Mainland Press, No. 4429 (June 4, 1969), 11-12. [IX]

―――. "Teaching Students to Study at a Higher Level for the Revolutionary Cause." April 21, 1969. Translated in Survey of China Mainland Press, No. 4408 (May 5, 1969), 5-7. [IX]

―――. "Worker-PLA Propaganda Team in Shihchiachuang No. 1 Middle School Conscientiously Carries Out Chairman Mao's Policy Toward Intellectuals." May 27, 1969. Translated in Survey of China Mainland Press, No. 4435 (June 12, 1969), 1-4. [VII]

Kuang-ming jih-pao [Kuangming Daily]. "Several Proposals in Connection with the 'Program.'" May 24, 1969. Translated in Survey of China Mainland Press, No. 4440 (June 20, 1969), 6-7. [IX]

LING, Ken [pseud]. The Revenge of Heaven: Journal of a Young Chinese. New York: G. P. Putnam's Sons, 1972. 413 pp. [XIII]

103

New China News Agency. "Draft Program for Primary and Middle Schools in Chinese Countryside. May 13, 1969. Reprinted in Survey of China Mainland Press, No. 4418 (May 19, 1969), 9-15. [IX]

————. "Primary, Secondary Schools Begin New School Year, Carry on Revolution." November 5, 1967. Translated in Survey of China Mainland Press, No. 4057 (November 8, 1967), 17-18. [V]

————. "Universities and Middle and Primary Schools Must Resume Classes While Making Revolution." October 24, 1967. Translated in Survey of China Mainland Press, No. 4049 (October 27, 1967), 1-3. [XIII]

VII. Teaching and teacher education

ALITTO, Susan Biele. "The Language Issue in Communist Chinese Education." Comparative Education Review, 13 (February 1969), 43-59.

"In addition to giving an historical perspective of the reform movement, this study probes into the political, social, and pedagogical problems of bringing the tools of literacy to one of the largest linguistic groupings in the world."

HU, Chang-tu. "Orthodoxy Over Historicity: The Teaching of History in Communist China." Comparative Education Review, 13 (February 1969), 2-19.

The author's "inquiry into the teaching of history up to the mid-1960s seems to confirm the view that ideological orthodoxy has taken precedence over historical scholarship and to show how history has been used to help achieve another cardinal goal, 'nationalism.' " He concludes, "as long as history is regarded as a powerful weapon for socialist revolution and history teaching as an integral part of political education historical scholarship in the traditional sense will continue to be denounced."

Hung-ch'i [Red Flag]. "A 'Mobile University' for the Training of Teachers with Greater, Faster, Better and More Economical Results — the Work Methods and Experience of Kwangtung Normal College's Mobile Tutorial Teams." No. 6 (June 1, 1971). Translated in Selections from China Mainland Magazines, No. 707-708 (June 28-July 6, 1971),

105

114-121. Appears also in Chinese Education, 5 (Spring-Summer 1972), 182-193.

"With a view to meeting the need for rapid development of educational services and breaking down the old rules and conventions, this College implements the educational policy of 'walking on two legs.' In succession, it organized a number of mobile tutorial teams and sent them deep into the countryside and mountainous regions, where they assist, in various forms, the different localities in training teachers. Immense results have been obtained, and at the same time, normal education has been closely combined with the Three Great Revolutionary Movements, thus promoting the revolutionization of the teachers" (Editor, Hung-ch'i).

————. "Strengthen the Building of the Ranks of Urban Primary and Middle School Teachers." No. 6 (June 1, 1971). Translated in Selections from China Mainland Magazines, No. 707-708 (June 28-July 6, 1971), 3-9. Appears also in Chinese Education, 5 (Spring-Summer 1972), 10-20.

"Emphasizes that to strengthen the building of the ranks of urban primary and middle school teachers we should, on the one hand, conscientiously select fine workers to join the ranks of teachers according to Chairman Mao's proletarian line; on the other, we should organize the original teachers to remold their world outlook in the practice of the Three Great Revolutionary Movements, correctly handle the relationship between the use and the reform of teachers and overcome the two deviations, i.e., using them without reforming them and reforming them without using them. In this process it is imperative to grasp the struggle between the two lines and the two world outlooks and to unfold revolutionary mass criticism in a deep-going and protracted manner" (Editor, Hung-ch'i).

Jen-min jih-pao [People's Daily]. "Carry Out Policy and

107

Rouse Enthusiasm of Middle and Primary School Teachers."
May 30, 1969. Translated in Survey of China Mainland
Press, No. 4435 (June 12, 1969), 5-8.

Reports how the 45 primary and middle school teachers
in government schools in Ts'ai-chia Kang Commune have
been remolded by poor and lower-middle peasants.

————. "Closely Follow Workers, Peasants and Soldiers in
Their Advance." January 6, 1969. Translated in Survey
of China Mainland Press, No. 4346 (January 27, 1969), 9-10.

Indicates that some rural school teachers regret having
gone to school and wasted time there, because they are
now receiving the same wages as illiterate peasants and
workers.

————. "Continuously Remold Old Ways of Thinking in the
Midst of Educational Revolution." June 8, 1969. Translated in Survey of China Mainland Press, No. 4438 (June
17, 1969), 5-7.

Reports that some students were still influenced by Liu
Shao-ch'i's doctrine of "going to school in order to become
an official" and consider themselves superior to the working class.

————. "Educate the Teachers and Students to Teach and
Learn Socialist Culture Well." June 21, 1969. Translated
in Survey of China Mainland Press, No. 4450 (July 8,
1969), 9-11.

Reveals how teachers are afraid that by paying due attention to "cultural subjects" they might be accused of following Liu Shao-ch'i's line of "intellectual development first,"
while some students look down upon "cultural subjects"
and would not attend "cultural" classes.

————. "Go Deep into the Realm of Teaching to Lead Reform

108

of Thinking." January 16, 1970. Translated in Survey of China Mainland Press, No. 4586 (January 28, 1970), 63-67.

A workers' propaganda team in Hunan holds that new text-books must be written in the midst of the "Three Great Revolutionary Movements" and that teaching must be done from the dialectical materialistic point of view.

————. "Proletarian Force of Teachers of a New Type Set Up in Shihchingshan Middle School, Peking." February 10, 1969. Translated in Survey of China Mainland Press, No. 4364 (February 26, 1969), 3-5.

Reports that the staff of teachers at Shihchingshan Middle School operated by a factory has been reformed by inviting advanced workers, peasants, and soldiers to give lessons in the school.

————. "Revolutionization of Teachers' Thinking Is a Question of Primary Importance." January 6, 1969. Translated in Survey of China Mainland Press, No. 4346 (January 27, 1969), 4-5.

Suggests that "poor and lower-middle peasants should help teachers heighten their awareness of the struggle be-tween the two lines, break with the counterrevolutionary revisionist line for education... and stand on the side of Chairman Mao's proletarian revolutionary line."

————. "Salaries of Rural Teachers May Be Paid by the People with State Aid." January 6, 1969. Translated in Survey of China Mainland Press, No. 4346 (January 27, 1969), 6-8.

Rural school teachers are to be paid by production bri-gades on more or less the same basis as peasants are paid, plus some allowance from the State.

————. "Unite With, Educate and Remold the Vast Majority

109

of Teachers." February 10, 1969. Translated in Survey of China Mainland Press, No. 4364 (February 26, 1969), 6-7.

The majority of teachers who are willing to integrate themselves with the workers, peasants, and soldiers, should be united, reeducated, and reformed.

————. "Worker-PLA Propaganda Team in Shihchiachuang No. 1 Middle School Conscientiously Carries Out Chairman Mao's Policy Toward Intellectuals." May 27, 1969. Translated in Survey of China Mainland Press, No. 4435 (June 12, 1969), 1-4.

Reports reeducation of teachers at the No. 1 Middle School of Shih-chia Chuang, Hopei Province, under the worker-PLA propaganda team.

Union Research Service. "Politico-Ideological Work Among School Teachers." 56 (August 29, 1969), 246-259.

A collection of reports dealing with activities of training and recruiting new teachers from among poor and lower-middle peasants and intensifying the politico-ideological work among teachers of primary and secondary schools.

WANG, Hsueh-wen. "Tang ch'ien ta-lu chiao-shih ti chu-ching" [Present Situation of Teachers in Mainland China]. Chung-kuo ta-lu yen-chiu [Mainland China Studies], 4 (April 25, 1971), 32-34.

Discusses the situation of teachers in China after reopening schools with special attention to the relationships between teachers and workers and PLA Mao Tse-tung thought propaganda teams, teachers and students, professional teachers and worker-peasant teachers.

WU, Ssu-chiu. "In Refutation of the 'Doctrine That Teaching School Is a Misfortune.'" Kuang-ming jih-pao [Kuangming Daily], June 21, 1969. Translated in Survey of China

110

Mainland Press, No. 4450 (July 8, 1969), 7-8.

Criticizes teachers for failing to see the great significance of the proletarian educational revolution and warns that if they persist in their view they will not be able to integrate themselves with workers, peasants, and soldiers.

See also:

Centre d'Etude du Sud-Est Asiatique et de l'Extreme Orient. "Education in Communist China." 2 vols. Brussels, Belgium, February 18-19, 1969. (Mimeographed) 245 pp. [IV]

FRASER, Stewart E. "Reforms for Rural Primary and Middle Schools." School & Society, 99 (April 1971), 237-241. [IX]

Hsin-hua-kung pao [New South China Engineering College Journal]. "The Black Program for Fostering Intellectual Aristocrats — Comment on the Ten-Year (1963-1973) Plan for Cultivation of Faculty Members for South China Engineering College." January 13, 1968. Translated in Survey of China Mainland Press, No. 4128 (February 29, 1968), 8-12. [VIII]

HUA, Lo-keng. "Learn Again to Dedicate Strength to Educational Revolution." Jen-min jih-pao [People's Daily], June 8, 1969. Translated in Survey of China Mainland Press, No. 4438 (June 17, 1969), 1-4. [XII]

Jen-min jih-pao [People's Daily]. "Chairman Mao's 'March 7' Directive Is the Beacon Light Guiding Us Forward." March 12, 1968. Translated in Current Background, No. 854 (May 24, 1968), 27-33. [XIV]

————. "'Education Program' Is Published in Good Time." May 19, 1969. Translated in Survey of China Mainland Press, No. 4429 (June 4, 1969), 9-10. [IX]

111

———. "Educational Program for Rural Middle and Primary Schools (Draft for Discussion)." May 12, 1969. Translated in Chinese Education, 2 (Winter 1969-70), 53-62. [IX]

Kuang-ming jih-pao [Kuangming Daily]. "A Good Measure for the Proletariat to Firmly Occupy Educational Positions." October 25, 1969. Translated in Survey of China Mainland Press, No. 4539 (November 18, 1969), 1-7. [IX]

———. "It Is Good for Poor and Lower-Middle Peasants to Go up the Teacher's Rostrum." January 25, 1969. Translated in Survey of China Mainland Press, No. 4360 (February 14, 1969), 1-3. [IX]

———. "A New Era of Poor and Lower-Middle Peasants Taking the Rostrum Has Begun." January 11, 1969. Translated in Survey of China Mainland Press, No. 4353 (February 5, 1969), 6-8. [IX]

———. "Propaganda Team in Hopei Normal University Helps University's Revolutionary Committee Further Carry Out Policy Toward Intellectuals." July 7, 1969. Translated in Survey of China Mainland Press, No. 4461 (July 24, 1969), 1-3. [VIII]

———. "Teachers and Students of Shantung Coal Mining College Study and Apply Chairman Mao's Works Flexibly." April 26, 1966. Translated in Survey of China Mainland Press, No. 3696 (May 12, 1966), 15-19. [VIII]

———. "Young Generals Ascend Teacher's Platform." November 18, 1969. Translated in Survey of China Mainland Press, No. 4549 (December 3, 1969), 1-8. [X]

LI, Chin-wei. Hung-wei-ping shih-lü [Facts About Red Guards]. 2nd ed. Hong Kong: World Overseas Chinese Society, 1968. 462 pp. [XIII]

112

———. Hung-wei-ping shu-pien [Supplement to Facts About Red Guards]. Taipei: National War College, 1970. 246 pp. [XIII]

NEE, Victor, and Don Layman. Cultural Revolution at Peking University. New York: Monthly Review Press, 1969. 91 pp. [VIII]

New China News Agency. "Draft Program for Primary and Middle Schools in Chinese Countryside." May 13, 1969. Reprinted in Survey of China Mainland Press, No. 4418 (May 19, 1969), 9-15. [IX]

———. "Ministry of Education Calls for Consolidation and Improvement of Farm-Study Schools and Agricultural Middle Schools," March 8, 1966. Translated in Survey of China Mainland Press, No. 3661 (March 21, 1966), 18-20 [IX]

———. "Universities and Middle and Primary Schools Must Resume Classes While Making Revolution." October 24, 1967. Translated in Survey of China Mainland Press, No. 4049 (October 27, 1967), 1-3. [XIII]

———. "Young Peking University Teachers Reveal Why Old Educational System Must Be Smashed." April 17, 1967. Translated in Survey of China Mainland Press, No. 3923 (April 20, 1967), 19-21. [VIII]

TSAI, Pei-hsun. "Use Material Dialectics to Handle the Relationship Between Character Reading and Teaching." Wen-tzu kai-ke [Written Language Reform], No. 3, (March 12, 1966). Translated in Selections from China Mainland Magazines, No. 529 (June 26, 1966), 32-35. [V]

WANG, Hsueh-wen. "Maoist 'Reeducation' of College Professors." Issues & Studies, 6 (February 1970), 7-10. [VIII]

VIII. Higher education

BRUCKNER, Lee Ira. "Spare-Time Higher Education in Communist China with Emphasis on Higher Correspondence Education." Unpublished Ph.D. dissertation, Montana State University, 1970. 282 pp.

Examines the development and nature of spare-time higher education in China (PRC) with special concentration on higher correspondence education. The major portion of the study pertains to the pre-Great Proletarian Cultural Revolution period.

Chiao-hsüeh p'i-p'an [Pedagogical Critique], August 20, 1967, published by the Editorial Committee of the Peking University Cultural Revolutionary Committee.

The issue contains "contributions by Red Guard groups in the Ministry of Higher Education" and at the time of publication was "the most comprehensive review of policy conflict in higher education." For a complete translation of this publication, see Chinese Sociology and Anthropology, 2 (Fall-Winter, 1969-70), 124 pp. This issue contains the following articles: "Supreme Directives"; A Commentator, "Thoroughly Destroy the Reactionary and Revisionist Educational Line of Liu [Shao-ch'i] and Teng [Hsiao-p'ing]"; The "Red Rock" Fighting Company, Peking Commune, Ministry of Higher Education; The "July 1" Fighting Company, Minister of Higher Education; The "Torch" Fighting Company, New Peking University Commune, "A Record of the Great Events in the Struggle Between the

114

Two Lines in the Field of Higher Education"; Second Class
of the Fifth Year Students, Department of Language and
Literature, Peking University, "Unveiling the Dark Side
of the Chinese Department's Professional Program in
Classical Studies"; "Welcoming the New High Tide of the
Great Educational Revolution"; "Educational Reform Activities in the Universities and Colleges"; Glossary.

China News Analysis. "An Episode of the Purge: K'uang Ya-
ming and Nanking University." No. 623 (August 5, 1966), 1-7.

————. "Higher Education." No. 816 (October 2, 1970), 1-7.

————. "In the Universities." No. 772 (September 5, 1969), 1-7.

————. "P'eng Chen, Peking, and Peking University." No. 615
(June 10, 1966), 1-7.

China Pictorial. "New Peking University Forges Ahead."
No. 6 (June 1970), 32-35.

Reports on the worker-PLA Mao Tse-tung thought propaganda team which has led the revolutionary teachers,
students, and staff members of Peking University in bringing about the revolutionary great alliance and "three-way"
combination, in carrying on revolutionary mass criticism,
in purifying the class ranks, and in consolidating and
building the Party.

————. "New Students with Practical Experience." No. 10
(October 1970), 40-43.

Reports how new students in Tsinghua University and
Peking University built their universities into bases for
a "three-in-one combination" of teaching, scientific research, and production by applying Mao Tse-tung thought.

————. "After the Period of Schooling Was Shortened." No. 20

115

(November 1971), 17-19.

A report on the Shenyang Medical College in the post-Cultural Revolution period. The period of schooling was reduced from six to three years.

FROLIC, B. Michael. "A Visit to Peking University — What the Cultural Revolution Was All About?" The New York Times Magazine (October 24, 1971), 29, 115-129.

The author, currently a research fellow at Harvard, has visited China twice during the past six years. The article reports on a visit to Peking University in July 1971. The history of this leading university during the period 1966 to 1971 was provided by Chou Pei-yuan, vice chairman of the Peking University Revolutionary Committee.

GUPTA, Krishna P. "Tsinghua Experience and Higher Education in China." China Report, 7 (January-February 1971), 2-14.

An analysis of Chinese Communist education from a socio-historical perspective, including a study of the background of educational reform during the Great Proletarian Cultural Revolution; a sociological case-study of the Tsinghua experience; a cross-cultural evaluation which isolates the specifically Chinese component of reform in the light of previous Communist theory and practice and the continuity and change in the Chinese pattern of higher education in the framework of the Mao-Liu controversy.

Hsin-hua-kung pao [New South China Engineering College Journal]. "The Black Program for Fostering Intellectual Aristocrats — Comment on the Ten-Year (1963-1973) Plan for Cultivation of Faculty Members for South China Engineering College." January 13, 1968. Translated in Survey of China Mainland Press, No. 4128 (February 29, 1968), 8-12.

116

This article condemns the Ten-Year Plan (1963-1973) for training of faculty members of South China Engineering College and claims it was aimed to train only "spiritual aristocrats" and "successors to the bourgeois cause" and that it runs counter to Mao's policy on proletarian education.

HU, Chang-tu. "The Chinese University: Target of the Cultural Revolution." Saturday Review, 50 (August 19, 1967), 52-54.

The author analyzes, throughout the initiation of the Great Proletarian Cultural Revolution in Peking University, the situation of universities in Communist China during the early phase of the GPCR and concludes: "As long as ideological purity is pursued with such single-mindedness within the Great Cultural Revolution, the pursuit of expertness through formal education in any form will suffer."

HUANG, I-chang, et al. "Smash Teng T'o's Conspiracy of Inciting Youths to Oppose the Party in the Cultural Revolution." Chung-kuo ch'ing-nien pao [Chinese Youth News], May 14, 1966. Translated in Survey of China Mainland Press, No. 3709 (June 1, 1966), 1-6.

Another attack against Teng T'o and Wu Han, written by nine college students in Peking.

Hung-ch'i [Red Flag]. "Minutes of a Forum in Shanghai on the Educational Revolution in Colleges of Science and Engineering." No. 8 (1970), 20-34. Translated in Chinese Education, 4 (Spring 1971), 36-63.

On June 2, 1970, Chang Ch'un-ch'iao and Yao Wen-yüan hosted a forum in Shanghai on the educational revolution in science and engineering colleges. This is the translation of the minutes.

―――. "The Reform in Education at Colleges of Science and Engineering as Viewed from the Struggle Between Two

Lines at the Shanghai Institute of Mechanical Engineering."
No. 3 (1968), 7-13. Translated in Chinese Education, 2
(Fall 1969), 3-14.

—————. "Reform Universities of Liberal Arts Through Revo-
lutionary Mass Criticism — Investigation Report on Futan
University's 'May 7' Experimental Liberal Arts Class."
No. 6 (June 1, 1971). Translated in Selections from China
Mainland Magazines, No. 707-708 (June 28-July 6, 1971),
89-99. Appears also in Chinese Education, 5 (Spring-
Summer 1972), 144-160.

"Dwells on the importance of revolutionary mass criticism
and social survey to the reform of universities of liberal
arts. Having conscientiously summed up their lesson in
traversing a tortuous path, Futan University's 'May 7'
experimental liberal arts class resolutely carried out
Chairman Mao's instruction, 'Liberal arts should take the
whole society as its factory,' and, centering on revolutionary mass criticism, organically combined classroom teaching and the Three Great Revolutionary Movements" (Editor,
Hung-ch'i).

—————. "Strive to Build a Socialist University of Science and
Engineering." No. 8 (1970), 5-19. Translated in Chinese
Education, 4 (Spring 1971), 7-35.

JACKSON-THOMAS, A., K. Janaka, and A. Manheim. "How It
All Started in Peking University." Eastern Horizon, 6
(May 1967), 19-31.

Jen-min jih-pao [People's Daily]. "Big Plot Exposed by a
Big-Character Paper Posed by Seven Comrades of Peking
University." June 2, 1966. Translated in Survey of China
Mainland Press, No. 3719 (June 16, 1966), 6-8.

A translation of the text of the big-character paper posted
by Nieh Yüan-tzu and six other members of the Department

118

of Philosophy, Peking University, on May 25, 1966, accusing Lu P'ing, Sung Shuo, and P'eng P'ei-yun of trying to check the mass struggle against Teng T'o and his group accused of being revisionists.

————. "Carry Out the Cultural Revolution Thoroughly and Transform the Educational System Completely." June 18, 1967. Translated in Current Background, No. 846 (February 8, 1968), 56 pp.

An official view of the change in methods of enrolling college students.

————. "Changing the World Outlook of Intellectuals Must Be Given First Place." April 11, 1966. Translated in Survey of China Mainland Press, No. 3683 (April 25, 1966), 6-9.

Report of the decisions made at a symposium on bringing politics to the fore in institutions of higher learning called by the Party Committee of the Ministry of Higher Education in Tsinan.

————. "Completely Carry Out Our Great Leader Chairman Mao's Latest Instruction, and Firmly Execute the Battle Order Issued by the Proletarian Headquarters." August 28, 1968. Translated in Chinese Education, 2 (Spring-Summer 1969), 18-25.

————. "Demolish the 'Little Treasure Pagoda' System of Revisionist Education." December 17, 1967. Translated in Survey of China Mainland Press, No. 4100 (January 16, 1968), 1-14.

Education for the elite was under severe attack, especially the eight-year course in medicine offered by Chinese Medical College, the former Peking Union Medical College aided by the Rockefeller Foundation before the Communist takeover.

119

————. "How Should Socialist Universities Be Operated?"
March 29, 1969. Translated in Chinese Education, 2
(Winter 1969-70), 14-26.

————. "How 'Socialist Universities' Should Be Run."
March 29-May 14, 1969. Translated in Current Background, No. 881 (May 26, 1969), 1-37.

The whole issue of Current Background comprises the
translations of all the articles in the series I to IV of the
discussion on how "socialist universities" should be run.

————. "More on How 'Socialist Universities' Should Be Run."
June 8-August 28, 1969. Translated in Current Background, No. 890 (September 18, 1969), 1-38.

A continuation of the discussion on how "socialist universities" should be run, series VI to X.

————. "Nanking University Exposes K'uang Ya-ming as an
Anti-Party, Anti-Socialist and Counter-revolutionary
Element." June 16, 1966. Translated in Survey of China
Mainland Press, No. 3726 (June 27, 1966), 1-5.

Reports how teachers and students of Nanking University
"struggled" against K'uang Ya-ming, the president of
the university.

————. "New Peking University Marches Forward in Big
Strides Along the Road Pointed Out by Chairman Mao."
September 16, 1968. Translated in Survey of China Main-
land Press, No. 4267 (September 27, 1968), 7-11.

An account of how members of Hsin Pei-ta Commune and
Chingkangshan — two rival Red Guard organizations of
Peking University — became friends again after the workers' Mao Tse-tung thought propaganda team came to
work in the university.

120

————. "Old System of Entrance Examination Must Be Changed." April 21, 1969. Translated in Survey of China Mainland Press, No. 4408 (May 5, 1969), 8-9.

————. "Peking Agricultural Labor University Studies Chairman Mao's Latest Instruction in a Big Way and Severely Repudiates China's Khrushchev's Revisionist Line for Education." September 6, 1968. Translated in Survey of China Mainland Press, No. 4260 (September 18, 1968), 1-2.

Denounces the "counter-revolutionary revisionist line of China's Khrushchev for education."

————. "Proposals to the Party Central Committee and Chairman Mao Concerning the Introduction of a Completely New Academic System of Arts Faculties in Universities." July 21, 1966. Translated in Survey of China Mainland Press, No. 3742 (July 20, 1966), 1-5.

Seven students of China People's University in a letter demand the "resolute, thorough and early smashing of old education system."

————. "Some Tentative Programs for Revolutionizing Education." November 3, 1967. Translated in Current Background, No. 846 (February 8, 1968), 25-28.

Contains the three proposals worked out by Tungchi University, Peking Forestry Institute, and Peking Normal University in accordance with Mao's May 7 directive.

————. "Tsinghua University Undergoes Great Changes Under Chairman Mao's Brilliant Idea, 'The Working Class Must Exercise Leadership Over Everything.'" May 9, 1969. Translated in Survey of China Mainland Press, No. 4423 (May 26, 1969), 1-6.

Discussion of ideological changes that have taken place in Tsinghua University under the leadership of the

121

Worker-PLA Mao Tse-tung Thought Propaganda Team.

————. "University Liberal Arts Colleges Should Institute
Mass Criticism and Repudiation as a Regular Subject in
the Curriculum." October 15, 1969. Translated in Survey
of China Mainland Press, No. 4527 (October 30, 1969), 1-3.

Urges that mass criticism and repudiation should form
part of the curriculum of liberal arts colleges so as to
change the thinking of teachers and students.

————. "The Way to Train Engineering and Technical Person-
nel as Viewed from the Shanghai Machine Tool Plant."
July 22, 1968, 1-2. Translated in Chinese Education, 2
(Spring-Summer 1969), 5-17.

————. "We Operated an Experimental Liberal Arts Class
for the Workers." October 15, 1969. Translated in Survey
of China Mainland Press, No. 4527 (October 30, 1969), 4-5.

Reports the establishment, operation, and activities of an
"experimental liberal arts class" which was set up in a
Shanghai factory in 1968.

————. "What Chairman Mao Says We Do." July 13, 1966.
Translated in Survey of China Mainland Press, No. 3748
(July 28, 1966), 12-14.

Two letters written by students of the Department of Law,
Hupei University, and the Department of Chinese, Peking
Normal College, which declare their support for educa-
tional reform.

————. "Working Class Must Firmly Grasp Leadership Power
of Education Revolution." March 29, 1969. Translated in
Survey of China Mainland Press, No. 4393 (April 11,
1969), 1-7.

Three articles, grouped together under the headline "How

122

Should Socialist Universities Be Run?", deal with measures for reforming college education.

KELLY, Maurice. "The Making of a Proletarian Intellectual: Higher Education and 'Cultural Revolution' in China." Current Scene, 4 (October 21, 1966), 1-17.

Kuang-ming jih-pao [Kuangming Daily]. "Advance on the Road of Revolutionization." December 23, 1968. Translated in Survey of China Mainland Press, No. 4337 (January 14, 1969), 1-4.

Reeducation of a group of university graduates and research fellows working at the Chinese Academy of Sciences.

————. "Arts Faculties Must Be Thoroughly Revolutionized." April 1, 1969. Translated in Survey of China Mainland Press, No. 4396 (April 16, 1969), 6-8.

Suggests: (1) leadership over the arts faculties must be vested in the working class; (2) students must be chosen from among those who are loyal to Mao, his thought, and his line; (3) arts faculties should be run after the pattern of the Yenan Anti-Japanese University.

————. "One Way to Reform Old Science Colleges." January 18, 1970. Translated in Survey of China Mainland Press, No. 4587 (January 29, 1970), 92-98.

Reports the establishment and operation of a "May 7" Chemical Factory in the Department of Chemistry, Northwest University.

————. "Propaganda Team in Changchiak'ou Medical College Warmly Helps Intellectuals to Creatively Study and Apply Mao Tse-tung's Thought." March 26, 1969. Translated in Survey of China Mainland Press, No. 4394 (April 14, 1969), 8-9.

Reports how the worker-PLA Mao Tse-tung thought

123

propaganda team stationed in Chang-chia-k'ou Medical College carried out Mao's teaching and reeducated the intellectuals of the college.

————. "Propaganda Team in Hopei Normal University Helps University's Revolutionary Committee Further Carry Out Policy Toward Intellectuals." July 7, 1969. Translated in Survey of China Mainland Press, No. 4461 (July 24, 1969), 1-3.

Reports how the worker-PLA Mao Tse-tung thought propaganda team stationed in Hopei Normal University carried out Mao's teaching and reeducated the intellectuals of the university.

————. "Re-Educating Intellectuals by Taking the Struggle Between the Two Lines as the Key Link." January 17, 1969. Translated in Survey of China Mainland Press, No. 4353 (February 5, 1969), 1-5.

Reeducation of a group of university students and postgraduates in a farm operated by a PLA unit since September 1968.

————. "Teachers and Students of Shantung Coal Mining College Study and Apply Chairman Mao's Works Flexibly." April 26, 1966. Translated in Survey of China Mainland Press, No. 3696 (May 12, 1966), 15-19.

Reports the reeducation of students and teachers at Shantung Coal Mining College.

————. "We Should Operate the Humanities University in the Style of the Anti-Japan Academy." April 1, 1969. Translated in Survey of China Mainland Press, No. 4397 (April 17, 1969), 1-3.

Suggests that the power over the Chinese People's University must be put in the hands of the working class, that

124

Mao Tse-tung's thought should command all, that the university should be run after the pattern of the Anti-Japan Academy of Yenan.

K'UNG, Fan. "Lu P'ing's Revisionist Educational Line and Its Evil Consequences." Jen-min jih-pao [People's Daily], July 19, 1966. Translated in Survey of China Mainland Press, No. 3751 (August 2, 1966), 13-20.

Condemns Lu P'ing's "revisionist, imperialist, and feudal" educational policy.

KUO, Ch'ao-t'ien. "Smash to Pieces the Bourgeois Educational System. Determine to Follow Revolutionary Ways." Chung-kuo ch'ing-nien [Chinese Youth], 13 (July 1, 1966), 16-17. Translated in Chinese Sociology and Anthropology, 1 (Fall 1968), 12-18.

LEE, Hwa-wei. "The Recent Educational Reform in Communist China." School & Society, 96 (November 9, 1968), 395-400.

Beginning with the three experimental plans of T'ungchi University, Shanghai; the Peking College for Forestry; and the Peking Normal University, the author traces back to the half-work, half-study school system before the Great Proletarian Cultural Revolution and analyzes the educational reform during 1967-1968. The educational standards, advanced study and research, military controls, and resistance to the reform are the major problems observed by the author.

LI, Ping-chang. "Ta-lu pu-fen kao-teng hsüeh-hsiao chaosheng fu-k'o" [Reopening of Partial Higher Educational Institutes on China Mainland]. Chung-kuo ta-lu yen-chiu [Mainland China Studies], 3 (April 10, 1971), 27-30.

Reports on reopening of higher educational institutes in

125

13 geographical localities: Peking, Hopei, Shantung, Shanghai, Kiangsu, Chekiang, Fukien, Anhwei, Hupei, Hunan, Kwangtung, Kwangsi, and Kirin.

LI, Yu-sheng, et al. "Letter to CCPCC and Chairman Mao." Jen-min jih-pao [People's Daily], July 12, 1966. Translated in Survey of China Mainland Press, No. 3742 (July 20, 1966), 1-5.

The letter, written by seven students of China People's University, suggests that the full course offered by arts faculties should be shortened, and students should be allowed to graduate ahead of time in order to participate in the Three Great Revolutionary Movements. Mao's works should be used as teaching material.

MARTIN, Charles M. "China: Future of the University." Bulletin of the Atomic Scientists, 27 (January 1971), 11-15.

NEE, Victor, and Don Layman. Cultural Revolution at Peking University. New York: Monthly Review Press, 1969. 91 pp.

Begun as a Master's thesis written by Victor Nee at Harvard, and later published as a special issue of Monthly Review in the summer of 1968. It traces the two styles of radicalism at Peking University during the Hundred Flowers and the Great Leap Forward and the growth of elitism in the first half of the 1960s, with a chronological account of the movement in Peking University from 1965 to the explosion of 1966. Several articles from the Peking Red Guard newspapers are appended.

New China News Agency. "Birth of Tungchi University's Tentative Program for Transforming Education." November 9, 1967. Reprinted in Survey of China Mainland Press, No. 4060 (November 15, 1967), 22-24.

Describes the tentative program for transforming the

126

education system worked out by the revolutionary students, teachers, and workers of the Shanghai Tungchi University. The program aims to turn the university into a three-in-one combination.

―――. "Early Results of Educational Revolution at Peking Institute of Physical Culture." November 29, 1967. Translated in Survey of China Mainland Press, No. 4071 (December 1, 1967), 11-12.

Peking Institute of Physical Culture, one of 10 such institutes in China (PRC), is trying out a number of revolutionary transformations in the field of physical education.

―――. "East China Teachers' University on Revolution in Education." November 28, 1967. Reprinted in Survey of China Mainland Press, No. 4070(November 30, 1967), 13-15.

This is a summary of an article in Jen-min jih-pao [People's Daily] entitled: Mao Tse-tung's Thought Illumines the Path of the Revolution in Education," contributed by the revolutionary committee of the East China Teacher's University in Shanghai. The article focuses on "repudiating the revisionist line in education."

―――. "How Peking Teachers' University Worked Out Program for Revolutionizing Education." November 21, 1967. Reprinted in Survey of China Mainland Press, No. 4066 (November 24, 1967), 16-18.

Describes how revolutionaries at the Peking Teachers' University worked out their tentative program for transforming education. This is one of the three tentative programs for transforming education.

―――. "Institutes of Higher Learning and Scientific Research Organs Will Soon Start Enrollment of Postgraduates for 1966." January 16, 1966. Translated in Survey of China

127

Mainland Press, No. 3625 (January 27, 1966).

————. "Jen-min jih-pao Features Tentative Programs for Transforming Education." November 3, 1967. Reprinted in Survey of China Mainland Press, No. 4057 (November 8, 1967), 8-10.

Summarizes three tentative programs for transforming education by Tungchi University, Shanghai; Peking Forestry Institute; and Peking Teachers' University.

————. "Nanking University Teachers, Students Condemn Counter-revolutionary Criminal Acts of Kuang Ya-ming." June 16, 1966. Reprinted in Survey of China Mainland Press, No. 3722 (June 21, 1966), 16-17.

Reports that a meeting held by teachers and students of Nanking University and delegates from other colleges in Nanking exposed and denounced the "counter-revolutionary criminal acts" of Kuang Ya-ming, the president of the university.

————. "Notice on Reform of Enrollment for China's Institutions of Higher Learning." June 18, 1966. Translated in Current Background, No. 846 (February 8, 1968), 1.

————. "Peking University Committee of CCP to Be Reorganized." June 3, 1966. Reprinted in Survey of China Mainland Press, No. 3714 (June 8, 1966), 11-12.

Describes the reorganization of Peking Municipal Committee of the Chinese Communist Party and the activities of the newly reorganized committee.

————. "Peking University Launches All-Out Criticism of 'China's Khrushchov.'" April 2, 1967. Reprinted in Survey of China Mainland Press, No. 3923 (April 20, 1967), 9-12.

128

Reports that the students and teachers of Peking University have thrown their full weight behind the campaign of criticism of the "No. 1 Party person in authority taking the capitalist road."

————. "Propaganda Team and Revolutionary Teachers and Students of Nank'ai University Conscientiously Implement Chairman Mao's Policy on Intellectuals." April 21, 1969. Translated in Survey of China Mainland Press, No. 4404 (April 29, 1969), 1-4.

Reports the struggle-criticism-transformation movement in Nank'ai University with the help of the workers' Mao Tse-tung thought propaganda team in the university.

————. "Students All Over China Voice Their Support for the Smashing of the Old Educational System." July 15, 1966. Translated in Survey of China Mainland Press, No. 3742 (July 20, 1966), 5-9.

Repercussions of the proposals by the seven students of the People's University.

————. "To Be Proletarian Revolutionaries or Bourgeois Royalists?" June 5, 1966. Reprinted in Survey of China Mainland Press, No. 3715 (June 9, 1966), 1-3.

An editorial of Jen-min jih-pao [People's Daily] attacks Lu P'ing and a small number of "bourgeois royalists" in Peking University.

————. "With 'Struggle Against Selfishness and Criticism and Repudiation of Revisionism' as the Key, Whip Up a New High Tide of Educational Revolution." October 29, 1967. Translated in Survey of China Mainland Press, No. 4060 (November 15, 1967), 13-21.

Recounts what the revolutionary teachers and students of Tungchi University of Shanghai accomplished in the period immediately following the resumption of classes in the middle of July 1967.

————. "Young Minority Teachers in Universities and Colleges of Sinkiang." May 8, 1966. Reprinted in Survey of China Mainland Press, No. 3696 (May 12, 1966), 19-20.

————. "Young Peking University Teachers Reveal Why Old Educational System Must Be Smashed." April 17, 1967. Translated in Survey of China Mainland Press, No. 3923 (April 20, 1967), 19-21.

An accusation against the former administrative personnel at Peking University who attempted to cultivate bourgeois intellectuals and, as a result, detested students of proletarian background who spent much time studying Mao's works.

ORLEANS, Leo A. "Medical Education and Manpower in Communist China." Comparative Education Review, 13 (February 1969), 20-42.

Through a case study, the author provides some insight into the state of technical education in general and the training of medical men in particular. He concludes that the effect of the Great Proletarian Cultural Revolution "will be little short of disastrous in its effect on China's educational system and particularly on the production of higher level medical personnel."

Peking Review. "Anniversary of Entry of Working Class into Realm of Superstructure." No. 31 (August 1, 1969), 3-7.

Discussion of the "achievements of China's first workers' and PLA men's Mao Tse-tung Thought Propaganda Team in Tsinghua University during the past year."

————. "Great Changes in Futan University Under the Leadership of the Working Class." No. 33 (August 15, 1969), 16-19.

130

――. "Industrial Worker Contingents Go into Colleges and Universities." No. 36 (September 6, 1968), 13-14.

――. "Marching Forward with Big Strides Under the Leadership of the Working Class." No. 31 (August 1, 1969), 10-13.

Concerns "the achievements of the revolutionary teachers and students of the Chunghshan Medical College, Kwangchow, led by the workers' and PLA men's Mao Tse-tung Thought Propaganda Team, in receiving reeducation by the poor and lower-middle peasants."

――. "Revolution in Education: Our Experience." No. 34 (August 20, 1971), 12-14; No. 36 (September 3, 1971), 17-18; No. 38 (September 17, 1971), 9-10.

Three articles in a series written by a student and two teachers of Tsinghua University, in which they discuss what they have learned in taking part in educational revolution. The articles also describe how some contradictions encountered were finally resolved.

――. "The Road for Training Engineering and Technical Personnel Indicated by the Shanghai Machine Tools Plant." No. 31 (August 2, 1968), 9-14.

――. "Tsinghua University's Intellectuals Advance Along the Road of Revolutionization." No. 14 (April 4, 1969), 10-12.

TS'UI, Min, Chang Wen-ch'ing, Ch'en Hsin-hsiu, and Kao Te-yuan. "Overthrow the Rule of Bourgeois 'Scholar-Tyrants.'" Jen-min jih-pao [People's Daily], June 6, 1966. Translated in Survey of China Mainland Press, No. 3722 (June 21, 1966), 12-15.

Four graduates of Peking University denounce Lu P'ing and P'eng P'ei-yun for having run Peking University in a bourgeois, reactionary way. They express support for the decision to dismiss Lu P'ing and P'eng P'ei-yun from their posts.

Union Research Service. "The 'Cultural Revolution' in Colleges and Universities." 44 (July 5, 1966), 17-29.

A collection of monitored radio reports dealing with the struggles against Chu Shao-t'ien, the first secretary of the Party Committee, Wuhan University, and Ho Ting-hua, the vice president of Wuhan University.

————. "Educational Reform After Resumption of Classes in Colleges." 48 (July 14, 1967), 42-56.

A collection of articles dealing with the conditions in colleges after the resumption of classes and their efforts in educational reform.

————. "Liu Shao-ch'i's Four Speeches Delivered at Peking College of Construction Engineering." 51 (April 26 and 30, 1968), 97-116.

Translation of four speeches of Liu Shao-ch'i made at the Peking College of Construction Engineering concerning the work team and antagonism between Party members and Youth League members in the college. Speeches were delivered between August 2 and 4, 1966.

————. "New Method of Enrolling Students in Institutes of Higher Learning." 44 (July 1, 1966), 1-16.

A collection of monitored radio reports containing opinions expressed by the students on the transformation of the existing educational system.

————. "Re-Education of College Teachers." 55 (June 13, 1969), 302-315.

A collection of monitored reports and press articles

132

concerning the reform of college education by applying
the policy of reeducation of intellectuals in order to push
forward the struggle-criticism-transformation campaign
in institutes of higher learning.

————. "Some Universities Are Recruiting New Students."
61 (October 2, 1970), 1-15.

A collection of monitored radio reports concerning activities of some provincial institutes of higher learning in
recruiting new students in the fall of 1970.

————. "The Worker Propaganda Teams Stationed in Universities and Colleges." 54 (January 10, 1969), 31-45.

Reports concerning the work of worker propaganda teams
in four universities and colleges: Shantung Agricultural
Mechanization College, Sian Metallurgical Construction
College, Kirin Agricultural University, and the South China
Technical College.

WANG, Chün. "Current Trends in the Reform of Higher Education in Communist China." Chung-kung yen-chiu
[Studies on Chinese Communism] Taipei, 3 (May 1969),
71-79. Translated in Chinese Education, 2 (Winter
1969-70), 27-52.

Analyzes the "socialist university" system in China (PRC)
through a synthetical study of the four proposals for experiments in 1968 (i.e. "The Road for Training Engineering and Technical Personnel Indicated by the Shanghai
Machine Tools Plant"; "The Revolution in Education in
Colleges of Science and Engineering as Reflected in the
Struggle Between the Two Lines at the Shanghai Institute
of Mechanical Engineering"; "From the Growth of Bare-
foot Doctors, a Look at the Direction of Reform of Medical Education"; and "Local Experts and the Revolution in
Agricultural Education") and the four special columns of
"People's Discussion" featured in Jen-min jih-pao

[People's Daily] on "How Should Socialist Universities Be Operated ?"

WANG, Ho. "Chung-kung tui Chien Po-tsan ti tsai p'i-p'an" [Chinese Communists' Recriticism of Chien Po-tsan]. Chung-kuo ta-lu yen-chiu [Mainland China Studies] , 2 (March 25, 1971), 34-36。

An analysis of recriticism campaign against Chien Po-tsan, a noted historian and former vice president of Peking University. The campaign was launched in Kuangming jih-pao [Kuangming Daily] in Peking on January 15, 1971.

WANG, Hsueh-wen。 "Initial Overview of the Maoist Transformation of Science-Engineering Schools." Issues & Studies, 6 (September 1970), 15-17.

A summary and analysis of two articles published in Hung ch'i [Red Flag], No. 8, July 21, 1970, entitled: "Strive to Build a Socialist University of Science and Engineering" and "Summary of the Forum on the Revolution in Education of Colleges of Science and Engineering in Shanghai."

————. "Maoist 'Reeducation' of College Professors." Issues & Studies, 6 (February 1970), 7-10.

A discussion and analysis of "reeducation" campaigns in Tsinghua University, Peking; Nankai University, Peking; Sun Yat-sen University, Canton; Peking Industrial College, and colleges in Shanghai.

————. "Maoist Reform of Universities of Arts." Issues & Studies, 6 (June 1970), 37-46.

Discusses and analyzes the evolving policy on the reform of the institutions of higher learning, reasons for the reform of universities of arts, ways and means of the

134

reform, resistance from teachers and students, and trends of the reform.

――――. "The Maoist Transformation of Science-Engineering Colleges." Issues & Studies, 7 (December 1970), 21-31.

Discusses and analyzes basic reasons of the reform; concept and models; contradictions and problems and future trends of transformation of science-engineering colleges during and after the Great Proletarian Cultural Revolution. Special attention is drawn to the Shanghai Forum on Revolution in Technical Colleges which was convened on June 2, 1970, in Shanghai by Chang Ch'un-ch'iao and Yao Wen-yüan.

WU, Chien-sung. "Ideology, Higher Education and Professional Manpower in Communist China, 1949-1969." Unpublished Ph.D. dissertation, University of New Mexico, 1971. 403 pp.

An investigation of the impact of Chinese Communist ideologies on higher education and professional manpower development and resistance to ideological enforcement during the period 1949 through 1969. Special attention is drawn to the reform of higher education during the Great Proletarian Cultural Revolution, the problems encountered, and the results.

Yang-cheng wan-pao [Canton Evening News]. "Destroy the 'Three-Family Village' Black Gang in Wuhan University." July 11, 1966. Translated in Survey of China Mainland Press, No. 3747 (July 27, 1966), 1-11.

Here Li Ta, president of Wuhan University, and two of his colleagues were charged with having "rabidly attacked the thought of Mao Tse-tung and promoted revisionist erroneous views." Together, they had also been opposed to the Party's leadership over institutions of higher learning.

――――. "The Fundamental Way to Solve the Problem of

135

Redness and Expertness Is Change the World Outlook."
April 13, 1966. Translated in Survey of China Mainland
Press, No. 3683 (April 25, 1966), 9-12.

A record of the debate held in Canton attended by teachers
and workers of 15 institutions of higher learning.

See also:

Centre d'Etude du Sud-Est Asiatique et de l'Extreme Orient.
"Education in Communist China." 2 vols. Brussels, Belgium, February 18-19, 1969. (Mimeographed) 245 pp. [IV]

CHANG, Yu-t'ien, Yang Yuan-huan, and Liu K'o-cheng. "Peking
Television University Is a Strong Fortress of the 'Three-
Family Village' Gangster Inn." Jen-min jih-pao [People's
Daily], June 11, 1966. Translated in Survey of China
Mainland Press, No. 3723 (June 22, 1966), 1-6. [XIII]

Hsin pei-ta [New Peking University]. Chinese Communist
Party, Central Committee. "(Draft) Provisions Concerning
the Current GPCR in Institutions of Higher Learning (for
Discussion and Trial Use)." March 14, 1967. Translated
in Current Background, No. 846 (February 8, 1968). [I]

Hung-ch'i [Red Flag]. "Consolidate the Leadership of the
Working Class Over the Revolution in Education." No. 6
(June 1, 1971). Translated in Selections from China Main-
land Magazines, No. 707-708 (June 28-July 6, 1971),
pp. 79-88. Appears also in Chinese Education, 5 (Spring-
Summer 1972), 128-143. [XII]

————. "Put Politics in Command, Persist in Integrating
Theory with Practice — A Report by the 'May 7' Commune
of T'ungchi University on the Situation of Revolutionary
Practice in Education." No. 6 (June 1, 1971). Translated
in Selections from China Mainland Magazines, No. 707-708

136

(June 28-July 6, 1971), 122-145. Appears also in Chinese Education, 5 (Spring-Summer 1972), 194-214. [XII]

———. "Reform of Teaching Material Is a Profound Ideological Revolution — Report on Reform of Teaching Material in Northern Communications University." No. 6 (June 1, 1971). Translated in Selections from China Mainland Magazines, No. 707-708 (June 28-July 6, 1971), 146-153. Appears also in Chinese Education, 5 (Spring-Summer 1972), 232-244. [XII]

Jen-min jih-pao [People's Daily]. "Combine Re-Education with Correct Use of Intellectuals." March 26, 1969. Translated in Survey of China Mainland Press, No. 4396 (April 16, 1969), 1-5. [XII]

New China News Agency. "Universities and Middle and Primary Schools Must Resume Classes While Making Revolution." October 24, 1967. Translated in Survey of China Mainland Press, No. 4049 (October 27, 1967), 1-3. [XIII]

Peking Review. "Revolution in Education Brings About New Outlook." No. 10 (March 7, 1969), 17-19. [XII]

UHALLEY, Stephen, Jr. "The Cultural Revolution and the Attack on the 'Three-Family Village.'" The China Quarterly, No. 27 (July-September 1966), 149-161. [III]

IX. Agricultural and rural education

FRASER, Stewart E. "Reforms for Rural Primary and Middle Schools." School & Society, 99 (April 1971), 237-241.

The author introduces a document, "Draft Program for Primary and Middle Schools in Chinese Countryside," released by Hsinhua News Agency, Weekly News (Peking), May 13, 1969. The author notes that "the draft program" is a result of studies undertaken in North China by the revolutionary committee of Lishu County in Kirin Province. The committee notes that this is a 'discussion draft,' and that a variety of people were involved in its formulation.

Hung-ch'i [Red Flag]. "The 'May 7' Directive Guides Us Ever to March Forward." No. 6 (June 1, 1971). Translated in Selections from China Mainland Magazines, No. 707-708 (June 28-July 6, 1971), 73-78. Appears also in Chinese Education, 5 (Spring-Summer 1972), 119-127.

"Introduces a typical case of the Army's agricultural production. It points out that when consciousness in implementing the 'May 7' directive is raised, the leadership strengthened, rational arrangements made, manpower adequately distributed, and the relationship between the leaders and the led fixed, it will not only obtain tremendous material results but what is still more important, it will effectively promote revolutionization of the Army and militancy in construction" (Editor, Hung-ch'i).

————. "A Network for Popularizing Socialist Education —

138

Report of an Investigation Conducted in Nanan Hsien, Fukien Province." No. 6 (June 1, 1971). Translated in Selections from China Mainland Magazines, No. 707-708 (June 28-July 6, 1971), 40-49. Appears also in Chinese Education, 5 (Spring-Summer 1972), 66-81.

"In Nanan hsien, schools are run in front of the doors of the poor and lower-middle peasants, in the remote mountain areas, and on the off-shore islands, as demanded by the poor and lower-middle peasants. This has changed the former irrational distribution of schools. Besides, spare-time schools and political evening schools of various types have been set up throughout this hsien by such means as are appropriate to the local conditions. In this way, popular education for school-age children and teenagers is basically achieved and 80 percent of the adult commune members can also take part in the study. Experience of this hsien shows that it is entirely possible to popularize socialist education so long as we conscientiously carry out Chairman Mao's 'May 7 Directive' and fully arouse the masses" (Editor, Hung-ch'i).

————. "Part-Work, Part-Study Education Trains New Men." 13 (December 6, 1965). Translated in Selections from China Mainland Magazines, No. 506 (January 10, 1966), 29-37.

Enumerates the advantages of the half-and-half system of education over the regular, full-time secondary schools. Current shortcomings of the part-work, part-study schools should be remedied by teaching reform; this hinges upon the revolutionization of teachers, who should become physical laborers at the same time.

————. "The Poor and Lower-Middle Peasants Have Acquired Socialist Culture." No. 8 (1970), 35-39. Translated in Chinese Education, 4 (Spring 1971), 64-73.

An investigative report on the rural educational revolution

by the Niu-t'ou-kou Brigade, Lin-t'ao County, Kansu
Province.

————. "The Revolution in Rural Education Must Be Depen-
dent Upon the Poor and Lower-Middle Peasants."
September 10, 1968, 27-31. Translated in Chinese Education, 2 (Spring-Summer 1969), 26-34.

————. "Run Spare-Time Education Well According to Chairman Mao's Directive — Report on an Investigation of Kao-
chialiukou Production Brigade of Chünan Hsien, Shantung."
No. 6 (June 1, 1971). Translated in Selections from China
Mainland Magazines, No. 707-708 (June 28-July 6, 1971),
27-39. Appears also in Chinese Education, 5 (Spring-
Summer 1972), 47-65.

"Presents a typical experience in upholding and developing
rural spare-time education in accordance with Chairman
Mao's proletarian educational line over the past decade
and more. Persisting in the correct direction of making
politics lead culture, they used a variety of forms of running schools that are suited to the peasants, compiling
teaching materials fitting in with local affairs, training
teachers and solving many important problems besetting
the development of the rural spare-time education. Five
texts of teaching material on local affairs are selected
and appended to this article for reference purposes"
(Editor, Hung-ch'i).

Jen-min jih-pao [People's Daily]. "'Education Program' Is
Published in Good Time." May 19, 1969. Translated in
Survey of China Mainland Press, No. 4429 (June 4,
1969), 9-10.

Comments on the "Draft Program for Primary and Middle
Schools in Chinese Countryside" of Lishu County, Kirin
Province. The Chinese text of the Program was published
in Jen-min jih-pao on May 12, 1969, and its English text

was released by New China News Agency, Peking, May 13, 1969.

—————. "Educational Program for Rural Middle and Primary Schools (Draft for Discussion)." May 12, 1969. Translated in Chinese Education, 2 (Winter 1969-70), 53-62.

Another translation of the "Draft Program for Primary and Middle Schools in Chinese Countryside" of Lishu County, Kirin Province.

—————. "A Few Proposals on the Question of Textbooks for Agricultural Middle Schools." May 8, 1969. Translated in Survey of China Mainland Press, No. 4419 (May 20, 1969), 10.

—————. "Forum on Entrusting Production Brigades to Run Primary Schools in the Countryside." November 14-December 7, 1968. Translated in Current Background, No. 869 (January 15, 1969), 1-35.

The entire Current Background issue contains selections of articles from the seven-part series concerning the operation of primary schools in the countryside appearing in Jen-min jih-pao.

—————. "How Poor and Lower-Middle Peasants are Managing Schools." October 24, 1968. Translated in Chinese Education, 1 (Winter 1968-69), 6-12.

An investigative report of the Kwangtung Provincial Revolutionary Committee on how poor and lower-middle peasants manage schools in the rural areas.

—————. "How We Compile New Textbooks." May 8, 1969. Translated in Survey of China Mainland Press, No. 4419 (May 20, 1969), 8-9.

—————. "An Important Front for Imbuing the Minds of Peasants with Socialist Ideas." January 16, 1970. Translated in Survey of China Mainland Press, No. 4585 (January 27, 1970), 31-38.

Reports the establishment of 18 political evening schools in a production brigade in Chekiang since June 1968 and their activities.

————. "Investigation Reports on Revolution in Rural Education." October 18-November 12, 1968. Translated in Current Background, No. 868 (December 31, 1968), 1-75.

Translations of 16 "investigation reports" on "revolution in rural education" appearing in Jen-min jih-pao. Each report concerns a representative example in one province except Chekiang Province, for which two examples have been given.

————. "Make It Convenient for Children of Poor and Lower-Middle Peasants to Go to School." May 19, 1969. Translated in Survey of China Mainland Press, No. 4429 (June 4, 1969), 13.

Comments on the "Draft Program for Primary and Middle Schools in Chinese Countryside" of Lishu County, Kirin Province.

————. "'May 7' Agricultural Senior Middle School Set Up in Commune in Honan." April 21, 1969. Translated in Survey of China Mainland Press, No. 4408 (May 5, 1969), 1-4.

It reports that in this school the old system of entrance examinations has been abolished and students are admitted by the recommendation of the poor and lower-middle peasants.

————. "Our Suggestions for Additions and Modifications to the Draft Education Program." May 19, 1969. Translated in Survey of China Mainland Press, No. 4429 (June 4, 1969), 14-15.

142

Comments on the "Draft Program for Primary and Middle Schools in Chinese Countryside" of Lishu County, Kirin Province.

————. "Our Views and Suggested Modifications." May 26, 1969. Translated in Survey of China Mainland Press, No. 4438 (June 17, 1969), 9-10.

Comments on the "Draft Program for Primary and Middle Schools in Chinese Countryside" of Lishu County, Kirin Province.

————. "School Management by Poor and Lower-Middle Peasants as Shown by the Practice of Three Production Brigades in the Educational Revolution." October 28, 1968. Translated in Chinese Education, 1 (Fall 1968), 3-14.

————. "Some Points of View Held by Us Poor and Lower-Middle Peasants." May 19, 1969. Translated in Survey of China Mainland Press, No. 4429 (June 4, 1969), 11-12.

Comments on the "Draft Program for Primary and Middle Schools in Chinese Countryside" of Lishu County, Kirin Province."

————. "Teaching Students to Study at a Higher Level for the Revolutionary Cause." April 21, 1969. Translated in Survey of China Mainland Press, No. 4408 (May 5, 1969), 5-7.

Suggestions concerning selection of students for junior middle school section of rural schools.

Kuang-ming jih-pao [Kuangming Daily]. "Agricultural School of a New Type Established and Managed by Poor and Lower-Middle Peasants." March 25, 1969. Translated in Survey of China Mainland Press, No. 4393 (April 11, 1969), 8-11.

Reports the establishment, operation, and activities of

143

the "May 7" Agricultural Academy which was set up in November 1968 by the poor and lower-middle peasants of I-ch'eng County, Shansi Province.

————. "A Commune Is Capable of Operating an Academy and Operating It Well." January 4, 1966. Translated in Survey of China Mainland Press, No. 3621 (January 20, 1966), 9-18.

Li-ming Academy, operated by a commune in a hsien of Kirin Province along the lines of the Communist Labor University in Kiangsi. Its enrollment, however, was only 158 in 1965.

————. "A Good Measure for the Proletariat to Firmly Occupy Educational Positions." October 25, 1969. Translated in Survey of China Mainland Press, No. 4539 (November 18, 1969), 1-7.

Reports that the "worker-peasant lecturers corps" have come to seize control of the schools in Tatung, Shansi Province.

————. "It is Good for Poor and Lower-Middle Peasants to Go Up the Teacher's Rostrum." January 25, 1969. Translated in Survey of China Mainland Press, No. 4360 (February 14, 1969), 1-3.

Reports that poor and lower-middle peasants of a production brigade in Yülin County, Kwangsi Province have taken the place of teachers in a primary school in the brigade and how they teach their pupils.

————. "'May 7' Agricultural School Is a Good Way to Revolutionize and Intellectualize the Laboring Peasants." February 28, 1969. Translated in Survey of China Mainland Press, No. 4380 (March 20, 1969), 5-8.

Reports the establishment and operation of a "May 7" agricultural school which was set up in November 1969

144

in Ch'ien-ts'un production brigade, Ching County,
Hopei Province.

———. "A Measure for Turning the Countryside into a Big
School of Mao Tse-tung's Thought." February 28, 1969.
Translated in Survey of China Mainland Press, No. 4380
(March 20, 1969), 1-4.

Reports the establishment and operation of "May 7" agricultural schools which were set up in Meit'an commune
of Kuch'eng County, Hupei Province.

———. "A New Era of Poor and Lower-Middle Peasants
Taking the Rostrum Has Begun." January 11, 1969. Trans-
lated in Survey of China Mainland Press, No. 4353
(February 5, 1969), 6-8.

Reports the formation of lecture groups of poor and lower-
middle peasants and their teaching in rural schools in
Feng-ch'iu County, Honan Province.

———. "Several Proposals in Connection with the 'Program.'"
May 24, 1969. Translated in Survey of China Mainland
Press, No. 4440 (June 20, 1969), 6-7.

Comments on the "Draft Program for Primary and Middle
Schools in Chinese Countryside" of Lishu County, Kirin
Province.

———. "With Cultural Power in Hand Peasants Should Compile Books." January 11, 1969. Translated in Survey of
China Mainland Press, No. 4353 (February 5, 1969), 9-12.

Reports how poor and lower-middle peasants wrote textbooks for primary school pupils in a production brigade.

New China News Agency. "Draft Program for Primary and
Middle Schools in Chinese Countryside." May 13, 1969.
Reprinted in Survey of China Mainland Press, No. 4418

(May 19, 1969), 9-15.

Official English text of the program. The original Chinese text of the program was drafted by the revolutionary committee of Lishu County, Kirin Province, and published in Jen-min jih-pao [People's Daily] on May 12, 1969, under the headline "discussion on turning state-run primary schools over to production brigades."

————. "Importance of Workers' Spare-Time Education Discussed at National Conference." June 14, 1966. Translated in Survey of China Mainland Press, No. 3721 (June 20, 1966), 18-20.

At the time when the Great Proletarian Cultural Revolution was surging to a new peak, workers' spare-time education was to help them master Mao Tse-tung's thought. Apparently, the two contending cliques were wooing the workers and attempting to gain control over them.

————. "Ministry of Education Calls for Consolidation and Improvement of Farm-Study Schools and Agricultural Middle Schools." March 8, 1966. Translated in Survey of China Mainland Press, No. 3661 (March 21, 1966), 18-20.

While reiterating the policies once adopted in 1958, the Ministry of Education called on all educational agencies in the country to establish a new force of teachers who have correct ideology and are willing to participate in productive labor.

Peking Review. "'Indigenous Expert' and the Revolution in Agricultural Education." No. 51 (December 20, 1968), 3-6.

————. "It Is Essential to Rely on the Poor and Lower-Middle Peasants in the Educational Revolution in the Countryside." No. 39 (September 27, 1968), 19-22.

A "report of an investigation into the experience gained

by the Shuiyuan Commune in Yingkou County in carrying out the revolution in education."

―――. "Nation's Revolutionary People Discuss Revolution in Rural Education." No. 51 (December 20, 1968), 7-10.

―――. "A New-Type School Where Theory Accords With Practice." No. 44 (November 1, 1968), 4-8.

An investigative report on the Wukou Part-Time Tea-Growing and Part-Time Study Middle School in Wuyuan County, Kiangsi Province.

―――. "Schools Managed by the Poor and Lower-Middle Peasants." No. 45 (November 8, 1968), 12-16.

See also:

Hung-ch'i [Red Flag]. "A Primary School Run by the People Under the Control of the Poor and Lower-Middle Peasants." No. 5 (1968), 46-51. Translated in Chinese Education, 2 (Fall 1969), 28-36. [V]

―――. "A Primary School Where Poor and Lower-Middle Peasants Hold Power." No. 5 (November 24, 1968). Translated in Selections from China Mainland Magazines, No. 638 (December 23, 1968), 15-19. [V]

Jen-min jih-pao [People's Daily]. "Carry Out Policy and Rouse Enthusiasm of Middle and Primary School Teachers." May 30, 1969. Translated in Survey of China Mainland Press, No. 4435 (June 12, 1969), 5-8. [VII]

―――. "Close to 500,000 Educated Youths in Shanghai Went to Mountain and Rural Areas in Past Year." December 23, 1969. Translated in Survey of China Mainland Press, No. 4572 (January 8, 1970), 132-134. [X]

147

―――. "Closely Follow Workers, Peasants and Soldiers in Their Advance." January 6, 1969. Translated in Survey of China Mainland Press, No. 4346 (January 27, 1969), 9-10. [VII]

―――. "Hungch'i Middle School in Penhsi, Liaoning, Forms Textbook Compiling Group." May 8, 1969. Translated in Survey of China Mainland Press, No. 4419 (May 20, 1969), 6-7. [VI]

―――. "Revolutionization of Teachers' Thinking Is a Question of Primary Importance." January 6, 1969. Translated in Survey of China Mainland Press, No. 4346 (January 27, 1969), 4-5. [VII]

―――. "Salaries of Rural Teachers May be Paid by the People with State Aid." January 6, 1969. Translated in Survey of China Mainland Press, No. 4346 (January 27, 1969), 6-8. [VII]

Union Research Service. "Public Primary Schools to be 'Sent Down' to Rural Production Brigades." 53 (December 31, 1968), 353-369. [V]

X. Youth and student affairs

GITTINGS, John. "A Red Guard Repents." Far Eastern Economic Review, 28 (July 10, 1969), 123-126.

ISRAEL, John. "The Red Guards in Historical Perspective: Continuity and Change in the Chinese Youth Movement." The China Quarterly, No. 30 (April-June 1967), 1-32.

Discusses the creation of the Red Guards; the Red Guards in action; manipulation, factionalism and opposition; the Red Guards in retreat, historical precedent; and some tentative observations.

Jen-min jih-pao [People's Daily]. "Close to 500,000 Educated Youths in Shanghai Went to Mountain and Rural Areas in Past Year." December 23, 1969. Translated in Survey of China Mainland Press, No. 4572 (January 8, 1970), 132-134.

Reports educated youths of Shanghai receiving reeducation from the poor and lower-middle peasants in mountain and rural areas in the Northwest, Inner Mongolia.

————. "Educated Youths Settling in a Commune in Inner Mongolia Actively Respond to Proposal of Not Returning to the City for the Spring Festival." January 30, 1969. Translated in Survey of China Mainland Press, No. 4360 (February 14, 1969), 4-5.

————. "Five Major Charges Against the Old Educational System." December 17, 1967. Translated in Survey of

150

China Mainland Press, No. 4100 (January 16, 1968), 9-11.

The Red Guard Corps of the No. 4 Middle School of Peking charges that the "old" educational system was guilty of (1) widening the gap between three classes; (2) separating students from the "three major revolutionary movements"; (3) imposing a bourgeois dictatorship on the working class; (4) encouraging young people to pursue personal gain; and (5) undermining the physical health of young students.

————. "It Is Not 'Useless' but 'Insufficient.'" May 15, 1969. Translated in Survey of China Mainland Press, No. 4423 (May 26, 1969), 13-14.

A refutation to the mood of students who considered their efforts had been wasted because they would be assigned jobs in rural areas.

Kuang-ming jih-pao [Kuangming Daily]. "Young Generals Ascend Teacher's Platform." November 18, 1969. Translated in Survey of China Mainland Press, No. 4549 (December 3, 1969), 1-8.

Reports how students are to play the role of teachers and to teach other students. The report also admits that the students chosen to teach have to be carefully prepared by the professional teachers for their role.

LEE, Pat-lo. "Unleashing the Youth." Far Eastern Economic Review, 57 (August 17, 1967), 327-331.

Life. "March on the Kremlin by Chinese Kick-outs: Last Chinese Students Evicted." 61 (November 11, 1966), 48.

MONTAPERTO, Ronald N. "The Origins of 'Generational Politics': Canton, 1966." Current Scene, 7 (June 1, 1969), 1-16.

"This article is based on the recollections of one student

leader (Dai Hsiao-ai) in Canton who was an active participant in school political affairs in mid-1966. It describes in some detail his view of the process by which Party authority in the schools was gradually eroded by student militancy and ultimately smashed by Red Guard attack."

New China News Agency. "Returned Student Tells of Soviet Persecutions." (Monitoring of Peking NCNA International Service in English, 2100 G.M.T., November 5, 1966), in Daily Report Far East, No. 217 (November 8, 1966).

New York Times [International edition]. "Peking Students Hailed as Heroes." February 2, 1967.

Peking Review. "Chinese Students' Valiant Struggle in Paris." No. 10 (February 3, 1967), 30.

————. "41 Red Hearts are with Chairman Mao Forever: Young Overseas Chinese' Heroic Struggle Against Indonesian Reaction," and "Paean to Mao Tse-tung's Thought From Overseas," No. 9 (December 16, 1966), 11-16 & 10.

REECE, Bob. "Students in China: China Revisited." Far Eastern Economic Review, 59 (March 7, 1968), 413-418.

The author, an Australian university student, visited China during 1967 and 1968; compares his impressions of two stages in the Great Proletarian Cultural Revolution and finds that the flamboyant enthusiasm of the year before, cooled by the factionalism of intervening twelve months, had given way to a much more sober mood.

SINGER, Martin. Educated Youth and the Cultural Revolution in China. Ann Arbor, Michigan: Center for Chinese Studies, the University of Michigan, 1971. 114 pp.

Briefly examines pertinent elements of the Maoist vision of society, and basic locii of discontent among educated young people on the eve of the Cultural Revolution. The main body of the essay is devoted to a relatively chronological review and reconstruction of the events of the Cultural Revolution as they affected young people. Finally, an attempt is made to summarize and integrate the data and to achieve a fuller understanding of educated young people's involvement in the Cultural Revolution.

SKOPINA, K. "Living and Study Conditions of Chinese Postgraduate Students at Voronezh State University, October 1965 Through October 1966," Komsomol'skaya Pravda [Komsomol Truth (Moscow)], December 20, 1966, 3. Joint Publications Research Service, Document 4954, (1967).

Ta-lu ch'ing-nien hsia-fang yün-tung ti yen-pien yü hou-kuo [The Transformation and Results of the Send-Down Movement of Mainland Chinese Youth] Taipei: Institute of Mainland China Affairs, 1970. 19 pp.

Discussions and analyses on the Send-Down or Rustification Movement of Chinese youth during the period 1964 to 1970.

TOWNSEND, James R. The Revolutionization of Chinese Youth: A Study of Chung-kuo ch'ing-nien. Berkeley: Center for Chinese Studies, University of California, 1967. 71 pp.

This monograph discusses formal problems related to the organization and role of Chung-kuo ch'ing-nien [Chinese Youth], the official semimonthly magazine of the Central Committee of the Communist Youth League, and examines the magazine's performance and the substantive issues by analyzing the contents of five different periods in the magazine's post-1949 history, namely, 1951, 1956, 1959, 1962, and 1965. The final chapter is devoted to the relevant events and the possibly damaging associations of the

153

Communist Youth League leadership and the downfall of
the magazine during the Great Proletarian Cultural
Revolution.

TSANG, Chiu-sam. "The Red Guards and the Great Proletarian
Cultural Revolution." Comparative Education 3 (June
1967), 195-205.

WANG, Wei-min, and Li I-chun. "Is It Useless to Study?"
Hung ch'i [Red Flag], No. 3-4 (date uncertain). Translated in Chinese Education, 1 (Winter 1968-69), 13-20.

Repudiates the theory that to study is to desire to become
an official.

WYLIE, Ray. "Red Guards Rebound." Far Eastern Economic
Review, 57 (September 7, 1967), 462-466.

See also:

Jen-min jih-pao [People's Daily]. "New Peking University
Marches Forward in Big Strides Along the Road Pointed
Out by Chairman Mao." September 16, 1968. Translated
in Survey of China Mainland Press, No. 4267 (September
27, 1968), 7-11. [VIII]

―――. "Students Should 'In Addition to Their Studies, Learn
Other Things.'" March 7, 1969. Translated in Survey of
China Mainland Press, No. 4383 (March 25, 1969),
9-10 [XIV]

Kuang-ming jih-pao [Kuangming Daily]. "Teachers and Students of Shantung Coal Mining College Study and Apply
Chairman Mao's Works Flexibly." April 26, 1966. Translated in Survey of China Mainland Press, No. 3696
(May 12, 1966), 15-19. [VIII]

154

MEHNERT, Klaus. Peking and the New Left: At Home and Abroad. Berkeley: Center for Chinese Studies, University of California, 1969. 156 pp. [XIII]

WANG, Hai-jung. "A Conversation with Mao," Atlas, 21 (January 1971), 42-44. [XIV]

WANG, Hsueh-wen. Chung-kung wen-hua ta-ke-ming yü hung-wei-ping [Chinese Communist Great Cultural Revolution and the Red Guards]. Taipei: Institute of International Relations, 1969. 734 pp. [XIII]

XI. International relations in education

The Age [Melbourne]. "Chinese Schools Closed: Books Burned, Russian Report." September 27, 1966.

CHEN, Yao-Kuang. "Yankee Imperialist Cultural Aggression in Asia and Africa." Peking Review, No. 9 (March 6, 1966), 15-18.

China News Analysis. "Foreign Policy: Rogue Elephant: Peking and the World: Futile Subversion," No. 672 (August 11, 1967), 1-7.

FEIFER, George. "Russia-Da: China-Nyet," The New York Times Magazine. December 4, 1966.

FRASER, Stewart E. "China's International, Cultural, and Educational Relations: With Selected Bibliography." Comparative Education Review, 13 (February 1969), 60-87.

Descriptive account of Chinese students who went abroad for their education both before and after 1949; with special attention to incidents arising during the Great Proletarian Cultural Revolution period as a result of the activity of students in Hungary, France, Iraq, and Czechoslovakia. The educational relationship between the Chinese and Soviet Communists is also discussed in detail. The most extensive bibliography on the subject to date is appended.

———. "Communist Education and Visiting Educators — Contrasts in Russian and Chinese Policy." Ninth lecture

156

in series Jennings Scholar Lectures 1966-67. Cleveland: The Educational Research Council of Greater Cleveland, 1968. Pp. 145-165.

An account of the treatment accorded to students, educators, and visiting scholars involved in the various programs of educational and cultural exchanges between China and the Soviet Union.

————. "Shattered Sino-Soviet Educational Relations." Phi Delta Kappan, 48 (February 1967), 288-293.

The author discusses and analyzes the situation of educational relations and cultural exchange programs between China and USSR during the early phase of the Great Proletarian Cultural Revolution with special attention to the case of "expulsion" of Chinese students who were studying in the Soviet Union.

————. "Sino-Soviet Educational Relations." Chapter 8 in Changing Dimensions in International Education. F. Robert Paulsen (Editor). Tucson, Arizona: The University of Arizona Press, 1969. 105-120.

Discussion of the varying nature of cultural and educational relations between China and USSR. (The account is an extension of the material developed above in Jennings Scholar Lectures.)

————. "Sino-Soviet Educational Relations: A Recent Episode." School & Society, 100 (January 1972), 54-58.

Similar to material in Jennings Scholar Lectures with minor revisions.

————. "U.S. International Education: The Chinese Communist View." International Educational and Cultural Exchange (Spring 1967), 74-81.

A brief introduction by the author affords an opportunity

157

to understand the Chinese Communist viewpoint, succinctly
presented by Chen Yao-kuang in Peking Review (March 6,
1966), entitled "Yankee Imperialist Cultural Aggression
in Asia and Africa." The writer skillfully uses principally
U.S. sources for a documented account of the "counter-
revolutionary aims" and "educational infiltration" as prac-
ticed by U.S. private and governmental agencies in developing international educational exchange programs.

KOVNER, Milton. "Communist China's Foreign Aid to Less-
Developed Countries," An Economic Profile of Mainland
Drive. (Studies Prepared for the Joint Economic Commit-
tee, Congress of the United States). Washington, D.C.:
U.S. Government Printing Office, 1967, 609-620.

New York Times. "Chinese and Russians in Melee at Lenin's
Tomb in Red Square" and "Chinese Students End Moscow
Visit." January 27, 1967.

Peking Review. "Absurd 'Academician.'" No. 10 (March 3,
1967), 28.

————. "Africa's Revolutionary People Unmask Renegade
Features of Soviet Revisionists as Accomplices of Imperialism." No. 11 (February 9, 1968), 25-27.

————. "Capitalist Restoration in the Soviet Union: Going all
out with a Revisionist Line in Education." No. 10
(November 3, 1967), 34-35.

————. "Capitalist Restoration in the Soviet Union: 'Liberali-
zation' and Westernization in Culture." No. 10
(November 3, 1967), 32-33.

————. "Chinese Communist Youth League Will Not Send
Delegation to Soviet Komsomol Congress." No. 9
(May 20, 1966), 20.

―――. "Chinese Students Beaten Up in Red Square: Chinese People Denounce Soviet Revisionists' Fascist Atrocities." No. 10 (February 3, 1967), 24-26.

―――. "Chinese Students in the Soviet Union Leave Moscow for Home." No. 9 (November 4, 1966), 36-38.

―――. "Chinese Students Studying in Hungary Return." No. 9 (December 9, 1966), 34, 35.

―――. "Counter Charges in Moscow." No. 10 (January 29, 1967).

―――. "The Desire of the Soviet People and the People of the World Over." No. 11 (March 9, 1968), 26-28.

―――. "Glimpses into the Soviet Revisionist Renegade Clique's Restoration of Capitalism." No. 11 (May 10, 1968), 28.

―――. "Hit Back Hard at the Rabid Provocations of the Filthy Soviet Revisionist Swine!" No. 10 (February 3, 1967), 23-24.

―――. "Moscow Suppresses Students Demonstration Against U.S. Embassy: Chinese Embassy Protest to the Soviet Government." No. 8 (March 12, 1965), 15-16.

―――. "Our Strong Protest." No. 9 (October 28, 1966), 11-12.

―――. "Peking Welcomes Anti-Revisionist Fighters Returned from the Soviet Union." No. 9 (November 11, 1966), 23-25.

―――. "Rotten to the Core." No. 11 (May 10, 1968), 27.

―――. "Soviet-Chinese Friendship Association Delegation Sabotages Friendly Relations." No. 9 (December 2, 1966), 29.

———. "Soviet People's Boundless Esteem for the Great Thought of Mao Tse-tung: Excerpts of Speech by Hu Teh-pao." No. 9 (November 25, 1966), 29-30.

———. "Soviet Revisionism Is One of the Biggest Foreign Exploiters in India." No. 10 (September 29, 1967), 28-29.

———. "Soviet Revisionism Robs Africa in the Name of 'Aid.'" No. 10 (September 29, 1967), 29, 39.

———. "Soviet Revisionism's Neo-Colonialist 'Aid.'" No. 10 (September 29, 1967), 26-28.

———. "Soviet Revisionist Crime Against Chinese Students in Iraq." No. 10 (February 3, 1967), 29-30.

———. "Soviet Revisionist Leading Clique Restores Capitalism." No. 9 (November 25, 1966), 27-29.

———. "The Soviet Revisionist Renegade Clique Is a New Pack of Vampires." No. 11 (May 10, 1968), 25-26.

———. "Soviet Revisionists Turn Truth Upside Down in Anti-China Clamour: Truth About the Suspension of Soviet-Chinese Friendship Association Delegation's Visit to China." No. 9 (December 23, 1966), 28-30.

———. "Soviet Union Is Not Qualified to Participate in African-Asian Conference." No. 8 (June 25, 1965), 7-10.

———. "Speeches of Students Returned from Soviet Union: Soviet Revisionist Renegades' Obstruction and Persecution Against Chinese Students." No. 9 (November 25, 1966), 25-27.

———. "'Stalin Group' in Soviet Union Acclaims China's Great Cultural Revolution." No. 11 (May 17, 1968), 20-23.

160

———. "Strongest and Most Vehement Protest Against Fanatic Suppression by Soviet Revisionists of Chinese Students Returning from Europe." No. 10 (February 3, 1967), 21-23.

———. "Strongest Protest Against Soviet Government's Unjustifiable Expulsion of all Chinese Students." No. 9 (October 28, 1966), 10-11.

———. "U.S. Global Strategy: Yankee Imperialist Cultural Aggression in Asia and Africa." No. 9 (March 4, 1966), 15-18.

———. "Wholeheartedly Serving the People of the World: Chinese Aid Personnel Abroad." No. 11 (March 15, 1968), 32-35.

Pravda [Moscow]. "Events in China." November 27, 1966. Reprinted in English edition Novosti. Moscow: Novosti Press Agency Publishing House, 1967.

TER-GRIGORYAN, A. "The Tragedy of China." New Times [Moscow], No. 10 (March 8, 1967), 9-12.

VAKHTIN, Boris. "Soviet Journalist Describes Visit to Communist China." Zhurnalist [Journalist (Moscow)], No. 1 (January 1967), 66-71. Translated in Joint Publications Research Service, Washington, D.C., No. 5383 (1967).

XII. Ideology and education

CHEN, Theodore Hsi-en. "The New Socialist Man." Comparative Education Review, 13 (February 1969), 88-95.

The author "seeks to delineate the image of the New Socialist Man — the modern version of the Confucian chun-tzu or Superior Man — as conceived by Mao and his followers, through a searching inquiry into the ideological inner source as well as an examination of the specific educational means by which the New Socialist Man is molded."

CHI, Fan-hsiu. "Ghost of Confucius' Shop and Actual Class Struggle." Peking Review, No. 50 (December 12, 1969), 18-21.

CHI, Wen-shun. "The Great Proletarian Cultural Revolution in Ideological Perspective." Asian Survey, 9 (August 1969), 563-579.

The article sets forth analytically the ideological issues that have been the main foci of debate in China. A contrast is drawn between the ideology that the Maoists attack and the ideology they wish to establish, including a discussion of the "two systems of education."

Chieh-fang-chün pao [Liberation Army Daily]. "Never Forget Class Struggle." May 4, 1966. Translated in Survey of China Mainland Press, No. 3696 (May 12, 1966), 5-10.

This editorial charged the "anti-Party, antisocialist"

162

elements, who were generally academic authorities, with acting in accord with imperialism, modern revisionism, and both foreign and domestic reactionaries. Members of the army should arm themselves with the theory of class struggle and resolutely fight against them.

HAN, Te-hou. "Intellectual Elements Must Be Correctly Appraised and Correctly Handled." Kuang-ming jih-pao [Kuang-ming Daily], March 26, 1969. Translated in Survey of China Mainland Press, No. 4394 (April 14, 1969), 6-7.

Most intellectuals, as the author has found, are neither pro- nor anti-Mao. They should be reeducated; therefore, they must not be pampered or discarded.

HUA, Lo-keng. "Learn Again to Dedicate Strength to Educational Revolution." Jen-min jih-pao [People's Daily], June 8, 1969. Translated in Survey of China Mainland Press, No. 4438 (June 17, 1969), 1-4.

The first of three self-criticisms that Hua Lo-keng made after the Great Proletarian Cultural Revolution (the second self-criticism of Hua was published in the November 1969 issue of China Reconstructs; the third one was published in Wen-hui pao, Hong Kong, on February 23, 1971). Hua, the director of the Institute of Mathematics, Academia Sinica, criticizes himself and denounces the "revisionist-roaders" for having tried to sacrifice him during the Great Proletarian Cultural Revolution in order to save their own skins.

Hung-ch'i [Red Flag], "Advance along the Glorious Path of Chairman Mao's 'July 21' Directive." No. 6 (June 1, 1971). Translated in Selections from China Mainland Magazines, No. 707-708 (June 28-July 6, 1971), 14-26. Appears also in Chinese Education, 5 (Spring-Summer 1972), 27-46.

"Shows that in the process of operating a school, it is

163

imperative to overcome the two kinds of one-sidedness —
to slight practice or to slight theory — pay attention to
enlarging the worker-students' basis of practice (from
the part to the whole, from proficiency in only one part
or work procedure to understanding the various processes
of production and their inter-relations), raise the worker-
students' theoretical level (by studying higher mathematics
and the relevant courses of vocational theory with problems in mind and on the basis of practice), promote the
unity of study and application, the particular and the general, theory and practice, and give impetus to technical
innovations" (Editor, Hung ch'i).

————. "Consolidate the Leadership of the Working Class
Over the Revolution in Education." No. 6 (June 1, 1971).
Translated in Selections from China Mainland Magazines,
No. 707-708 (June 28-July 6, 1971), 79-88. Appears also
in Chinese Education, 5 (Spring-Summer 1972), 128-143.

"Discusses the way in which to build a leading body. In
places where the intellectuals and the worker-peasant-
soldier students form the principal objects of work, how
to raise the leading body's consciousness in line, enforce
the mass line and carry out the Party policy so as to consolidate further the political leadership of the working
class is a key question bearing on carrying the revolution
in education through to the end along Chairman Mao's
revolutionary line" (Editor, Hung-ch'i).

————. "Put Politics in Command, Persist in Integrating
Theory with Practice — A Report by the 'May 7' Commune
of T'ungchi University on the Situation of Revolutionary
Practice in Education." No. 6 (June 1, 1971). Translated
in Selections from China Mainland Magazines, No. 707-
708 (June 28-July 6, 1971), 122-145. Appears also in
Chinese Education, 5 (Spring-Summer 1972), 194-214.

"The first part of this article sums up the experience

164

gained in ideological and political work for the worker-
peasant-soldier students and explains the importance of
giving prominence to proletarian politics. The second
part sums up how the unity of theory and practice is promoted in the process of linking up teaching with typical
engineering work. This means selecting representative
engineering work on the basis of the need of teaching and
in accordance with the principle of proceeding from the
shallow to the deep and from the easy to the difficult, and
through such links as construction work, designing and
teaching of theory, linking participation in practice with
teaching of theory, and striving to obtain more complete
knowledge. The third part deals with the question of
building a 'three-in-one' combination teaching force"
(Editor, Hung-ch'i).

————. "Reform of Teaching Material Is a Profound Ideological Revolution — Report on Reform of Teaching Material
in Northern Communications University." No. 6 (June 1,
1971). Translated in Selections from China Mainland
Magazines, No. 707-708 (June 28-July 6, 1971), 146-153.
Appears also in Chinese Education, 5 (Spring-Summer
1972), 232-244.

"Reform of teaching material is a profound ideological
revolution. It is first necessary to have a correct political direction, solve the question of "writing books for
whom," and, under the Party's leadership, form a three-
way compiling group of workers, technical personnel, and
teachers so as to gradually promote the integration of
theory and practice. In the course of compiling, it is imperative to analyze problems from the viewpoint of one
dividing into two, to overcome the two kinds of one-
sidedness of affirming everything and negating everything,
to be less but finer in content, to resolutely remove scho-
lastic philosophy, and to strive to spread the advanced
experiences" (Editor, Hung-ch'i).

165

————. "Train Workers to Have Socialist Consciousness and Culture." No. 8 (1970), 40-45. Translated in Chinese Education, 4 (Spring 1971), 74-85.

Jen-min jih-pao [People's Daily]. "Care Must Be Exercised to Prevent the Development of Two Tendencies While Making Arrangements for Political and Language Classes." June 21, 1969. Translated in Survey of China Mainland Press, No. 4450 (July 8, 1969), 12-13.

Suggests that in teaching "political language" in primary schools, more time should be devoted to the teaching of fundamental knowledge of language. The article also contains other suggestions for educational reform.

————. "Combine Re-Education with Correct Use of Intellectuals." March 26, 1969. Translated in Survey of China Mainland Press, No. 4396 (April 16, 1969), 1-5.

Reeducation of the intellectual elements at Changchun Biological Products Institute.

————. "Do We Need Foreign Language Courses?" March 7, 1969. Translated in Survey of China Mainland Press, No. 4383 (March 25, 1969), 11.

Argues that foreign language courses are necessary because it is necessary to propagate Marxism-Leninism and the thought of Mao Tse-tung among people of the whole world.

————. "Our Views on the Curriculum." May 26, 1969. Translated in Survey of China Mainland Press, No. 4438 (June 17, 1969), 8.

Suggests that Chinese and world histories be rewritten from the viewpoint of class struggle.

————. "Overcome Tendency of Overlooking Cultural and

166

Educational Fronts, Continuously Push Forward Revolution of Education." June 9, 1969. Translated in Survey of China Mainland Press, No. 4444 (June 26, 1969), 7-10.

The article warns that "class enemies" were still able to sabotage attempts at educational revolution.

KAO, Hsia. "Criticize Revisionism and Rectify Our Work Style to Win New Victories in Educational Revolution. Hung-ch'i [Red Flag], No. 6 (June 1, 1971). Translated in Selections from China Mainland Magazines, No. 707-708 (June 28-July 6, 1971), 10-14. Appears also in Chinese Education, 5 (Spring-Summer 1972), 21-26.

"Stresses the importance of continuously developing revolutionary mass criticism and keeping a good grip on the struggle between the two classes, the two roads, and the two lines in order to win new victories in the revolution in education" (Editor, Hung-ch'i).

Kuang-ming jih-pao [Kuangming Daily]. "A Good Experience in Educational Revolution." November 18, 1969. Translated in Survey of China Mainland Press, No. 4549 (December 3, 1969), 9-11.

The system of making students teach other students is praised in this article as having far-reaching significance to foster successors to the proletarian revolutionary cause.

————. "Intellectual Elements Must Be Correctly Appraised and Correctly Handled." March 26, 1969. Translated in Survey of China Mainland Press, No. 4394 (April 14, 1969), 6-7.

Reveals that there are two erroneous tendencies in carrying out the reeducation of intellectuals: (1) regarding all intellectuals as beyond salvage and wanting to discard them altogether; (2) wanting to pamper the intellectuals modestly instead of imposing strict demands on them.

167

————. "Revolution in Art Education as Seen from Growth of 'Red Painter-Soldiers.'" April 14, 1969. Translated in Survey of China Mainland Press, No. 4408 (May 5, 1969), 10-15.

Reports the needs, the training, and the work of Red Painter-Soldiers" — artists of worker, peasant, or soldier origin — from the Great Proletarian Cultural Revolution.

————. "Working Class Must Lead Schools and Colleges Forever." April 1, 1969. Translated in Survey of China Mainland Press, No. 4394 (April 14, 1969), 4-5.

The article advocates that the working class must liberate science and technology from the monopoly of bourgeois intellectuals.

Peking Review. "A Criticism of Confucius' Thinking on Education." No. 38 (September 17, 1971), 6-9.

Repudiates the suggestion that "a good scholar will make a good official" and relates Liu Shao-ch'i' to the "counter-revolutionary revisionist line in education."

————. "Revolution in Education Brings About New Outlook." No. 10 (March 7, 1969), 17-19.

"The Revolution in Education in Colleges of Science and Engineering as Reflected in the Struggle Between the Two Lines at the Shanghai Institute of Mechanical Engineering." No. 37 (September 13, 1968), 13-17.

————. "Running the School for Training Successors to the Revolutionary Cause of the Proletariat." No. 47 (November 2, 1968), 7-9, 28.

————. "A Vanguard Fighter Who Dedicated His Life to the Proletarian Educational Revolution." No. 34 (August 22, 1969), 14-18.

SEYMOUR, James Dulles. "The Policies of the Chinese Communists Toward China's Intellectuals and Professionals." Unpublished Ph.D. dissertation, Columbia University, 1968. 318 pp.

Surveys the history of the relations between the Chinese Communist Party and the intelligentsia from its earliest days to the period of the Great Proletarian Cultural Revolution.

WANG, Hsueh-wen. "Ten Contradictions in the Maoist Educational Revolution." Issues & Studies, 8 (October 1971), 45-60.

Enumerates and analyzes ten contradictions in Chinese Communist educational revolution: (1) between politics and vocational study; (2) between leadership and masses, between unity and struggle; (3) between destruction and construction, between "revolutionary mass criticism" and "compiling of new teaching materials"; (4) between study and learning other things; (5) between theory and practice, between book knowledge and practical knowledge; (6) between the use and the reform of teachers; (7) between popularization and raising standards; (8) between "running schools through diligence and frugality" and "state aid"; (9) between classroom and society, between the activities carried out inside and outside the school; (10) between the educational front and other fronts.

See also:

BASTID, Marianne. "Economic Necessity and Political Ideals in Educational Reform During the Cultural Revolution." The China Quarterly, No. 42 (April-June 1970), 16-45. [IV]

BOHLEN, Charles. "Education in China: Studies in Maoism." Far Eastern Economic Review, 67 (February 19, 1970), 19-22. [IV]

BRIDGHAM, Phillip. "Mao's 'Culture Revolution': Origin and Development." The China Quarterly, No. 29 (January-March, 1967), 1-35. [III]

Centre d'Etude du Sud-Est Asiatique et de l'Extreme Orient. "Education in Communist China." 2 vols. Brussels, Belgium, February 18-19, 1969. (Mimeographed) 245 pp. [IV]

Chiao-yü ke-ming [Educational Revolution]. "Chronology of the Two-Road Struggle on the Educational Front in the Past Seventeen Years." May 6, 1967. Translated in Chinese Education, 1 (Spring 1968), 3-58. [IV]

FANN, K. T. "Philosophy in the Chinese Cultural Revolution." International Philosophical Quarterly, 9 (September 1969), 449-459. [III]

HSIAO, Gene T. "The Background and Development of 'The Proletarian Cultural Revolution.'" Asian Survey, 7 (June 1967), 389-404. [III]

HSUAN, Wei-tung. "Put Mao Tse-tung's Thought in Command of Kindergarten Education." Kuang-ming jih-pao [Kuang-ming Daily], March 31, 1969. Translated in Survey of China Mainland Press, No. 4400 (April 23, 1969), 1-6. [V]

HU, Chang-tu, ed. Aspects of Chinese Education. New York: Teachers College, Columbia University, 1969. 95 pp. [IV]

HU, Chang-tu. "Orthodoxy Over Historicity: The Teaching of History in Communist China." Comparative Education Review, 13 (February 1969), 2-19. [VII]

Hung-ch'i [Red Flag]. "A New Type of School That Combines Theory with Practice." No. 4 (1968), 24-31. Translated in Chinese Education, 2 (Fall 1969), 15-27. [I]

170

―――. "The Poor and Lower-Middle Peasants Have Acquired
Socialist Culture." No. 8 (1970), 35-39. Translated in
Chinese Education, 4 (Spring 1971), 64-73. [IX]

Jen-min jih-pao [People's Daily]. "Changing the World Outlook of Intellectuals Must Be Given First Place." April 11,
1966. Translated in Survey of China Mainland Press,
No. 3683 (April 25, 1966), 6-9. [VIII]

―――. "Continuously Remold Old Ways of Thinking in the
Midst of Educational Revolution." June 8, 1969. Translated
in Survey of China Mainland Press, No. 4438 (June 17,
1969), 5-7. [VII]

―――. "Educate the Teachers and Students to Teach and
Learn Socialist Culture Well." June 21, 1969. Translated
in Survey of China Mainland Press, No. 4450 (July 8,
1969), 9-11. [VII]

―――. "Go Deep into the Realm of Teaching to Lead Reform
of Thinking." January 16, 1970. Translated in Survey of
China Mainland Press, No. 4586 (January 28, 1970),
63-67. [VII]

―――. "How 'Socialist Universities' Should Be Run."
March 29-May 14, 1969. Translated in Current Background, No. 881 (May 26, 1969), 1-37. [VIII]

―――. "An Important Front for Imbuing the Minds of Peasants with Socialist Ideas." January 16, 1970. Translated
in Survey of China Mainland Press, No. 4585 (January 27,
1970), 31-38. [IX]

―――. "Peking Agricultural Labor University Studies Chair-
man Mao's Latest Instruction in a Big Way and Severely
Repudiates China's Khrushchev's Revisionist Line for
Education." September 6, 1968. Translated in Survey of

China Mainland Press, No. 4260 (September 18, 1968), 1-2. [VIII]

———. "The Red Sun Rises in the Hearts of the Red Young Fighters." March 11, 1968. Translated in Current Background, No. 845 (May 24, 1968), 25-26. [V]

———. "Shorten the Period of Schooling and Revolutionize Education." January 9, 1968. Translated in Chinese Education, 1 (Summer 1968), 63-67. [XIII]

———. "Students Should 'In Addition to Their Studies, Learn Other Things.'" March 7, 1969. Translated in Survey of China Mainland Press, No. 4383 (March 25, 1969), 9-10. [XIV]

———. "Tear Aside the Bourgeois Mask of 'Liberty, Equality and Fraternity.'" June 4, 1966. Translated in Survey of China Mainland Press, No. 3714 (June 8, 1966), 1-8. [III]

———. "Tsinghua University Undergoes Great Changes Under Chairman Mao's Brilliant Idea, 'The Working Class Must Exercise Leadership over Everything.'" May 9, 1969. Translated in Survey of China Mainland Press, No. 4423 (May 26, 1969), 1-6. [VIII]

———. "Unite With, Educate and Remold the Vast Majority of Teachers." February 10, 1969. Translated in Survey of China Mainland Press, No. 4364 (February 26, 1969), 6-7. [VII]

———. "University Liberal Arts Colleges Should Institute Mass Criticism and Repudiation as a Regular Subject in the Curriculum." October 15, 1969. Translated in Survey of China Mainland Press, No. 4527 (October 30, 1969), 1-3. [VIII]

———. "Working Class Must Firmly Grasp Leadership Power

172

of Education Revolution." March 29, 1969. Translated in Survey of China Mainland Press, No. 4393 (April 11, 1969), 1-7. [VIII]

Kuang-ming jih-pao [Kuangming Daily]. "Arts Faculties Must Be Thoroughly Revolutionized." April 1, 1969. Translated in Survey of China Mainland Press, No. 4396 (April 16, 1969), 6-8. [VIII]

————. "Bold Experiments in Pedagogic Reform." January 25, 1969. Translated in Survey of China Mainland Press, No. 4359 (February 13, 1969), 6-8. [VI]

————. "Propaganda Team in Changchiak'ou Medical College Warmly Helps Intellectuals to Creatively Study and Apply Mao Tse-tung's Thought." March 26, 1969. Translated in Survey of China Mainland Press, No. 4394 (April 14, 1969), 8-9. [VIII]

————. "Propaganda Team in Hopei Normal University Helps University's Revolutionary Committee Further Carry Out Policy Toward Intellectuals." July 7, 1969. Translated in Survey of China Mainland Press, No. 4461 (July 24, 1969), 1-3. [VIII]

————. "Re-Educating Intellectuals by Taking the Struggle Between the Two Lines as the Key Link." January 17, 1969. Translated in Survey of China Mainland Press, No. 4353 (February 5, 1969), 1-5. [VIII]

————. "Resolutely Implement Chairman Mao's Directive on Resumption of Classes to Make Revolution." April 23, 1969. Translated in Survey of China Mainland Press, No. 4409 (May 6, 1969), 6-10. [VI]

————. "We Should Operate the Humanities University in the Style of the Anti-Japan Academy." April 1, 1969.

173

Translated in Survey of China Mainland Press, No. 4397
(April 17, 1969), 1-3. [VIII]

LI, Ting-sheng. The CCP's Persecution of Chinese Intellectuals in 1949-69. Taipei: Asian People's Anti-Communist
League, 1969. 67 pp. [II]

New China News Agency. "Propaganda Team and Revolutionary
Teachers and Students of Nank'ai University Conscientious-
ly Implement Chairman Mao's Policy on Intellectuals."
April 21, 1969. Translated in Survey of China Mainland
Press, No. 4404 (April 29, 1969), 1-4. [VIII]

Peking Review. "Anniversary of Entry of Working Class into
Realm of Superstructure." 31 (August 1, 1969), 3-7. [VIII]

PUSEY, James R. Wu Han: Attacking the Present Through the
Past. Cambridge, Mass.: East Asian Research Center,
Harvard University, 1969. 84 pp. [III]

SCHURMANN, Herbert Franz. Ideology and Organization in
Communist China. 2d ed. Berkeley: University of California Press, 1968. 642 pp. [II]

SCHWARTZ, Benjamin I. Communism and China: Ideology in
Flux. Cambridge, Mass.: Harvard University Press,
1968. 254 pp. [II]

SHIH, Yen-hung. "Down With the Fountainhead of Revisionist
Education." Jen-min jih-pao [People's Daily], July 18,
1967. Translated in Chinese Education, 1 (Summer 1968),
16-31. [XIII]

TOWNSEND, James R. Political Participation in Communist
China. Berkeley: University of California Press, 1969.
233 pp. [II]

174

————. The Revolutionization of Chinese Youth: A Study of Chung-kuo ch'ing-nien. Berkeley: Center for Chinese Studies, University of California, 1967. 71 pp. [X]

Union Research Service. "Politico-Ideological Work Among School Teachers." 56 (August 29, 1969), 246-259. [VII]

————. "Re-Education of College Teachers." 55 (June 13, 1969), 302-315. [VIII]

————. "Reports on Educational Reform and Criticism Against Liu Shao-ch'i's 'Dual Educational System.' " 50 (March 8, 1968), 241-255. [XIII]

WANG, Chang-ling. Chung-kung ti wen-i cheng-feng [Chinese Communist Rectification in Literature and Art Fields]. Taipei: Institute of International Relations, 1967. 264 pp. [II]

WANG, Ho. "Chung-kung tui Chien Po-tsan ti tsai p'i-p'an" [Chinese Communists' Recriticism of Chien Po-tsan]. Chung-kuo ta-lu yen-chiu [Mainland China Studies], 2 (March 25, 1971), 34-36. [VIII]

WANG, Hsueh-wen. "Tang ch'ien ta-lu chiao-shih ti chu-ching" [Present Situation of Teachers in Mainland China]. Chung-kuo ta-lu yen-chiu [Mainland China Studies], 4 (April 25, 1971), 32-34. [VII]

WANG, Wei-min, and Li I-chun. "Is It Useless to Study?" Hung ch'i [Red Flag], No. 3-4 (date uncertain). Translated in Chinese Education, 1 (Winter 1968-69), 13-20. [X]

WU, Chien-sung. "Ideology, Higher Education and Professional Manpower in Communist China, 1949-1969." Unpublished Ph.D. dissertation, University of New Mexico, 1971. 403 pp. [VIII]

175

WU, Ssu-chiu. "In Refutation of the 'Doctrine That Teaching School Is a Misfortune.'" Kuang-ming jih-pao [Kuangming Daily], June 21, 1969. Translated in Survey of China Mainland Press, No. 4450 (July 8, 1969), 7-8. [VII]

Yang-cheng wan-pao [Canton Evening News]. "The Fundamental Way to Solve the Problem of Redness and Expertness Is Change the World Outlook." April 13, 1966. Translated in Survey of China Mainland Press, No. 3683 (April 25, 1966), 9-12. [VIII]

XIII. Educational development and the Great Proletarian Cultural Revolution (1966-1968)

BENNETT, Gordon A., and Ronald N. Montaperto. Red Guard: The Political Biography of Dai Hsiao-ai. New York: Doubleday, 1971. 267 pp.

An account of the Great Proletarian Cultural Revolution as viewed through the biography of Dai Hsiao-ai, a Red Guard and student activist leader in the city of Canton. Told in great part in Dai's own words, this Red Guard traces his initial enthusiasm for Mao's Revolution, his trips across China to mass demonstrations in Peking, his growing role as a faction leader, and the ultimate disillusionment that led him to leave his family and comrades behind and seek refuge in Hong Kong.

CHANG, Yu-t'ien, Yang Yuan-huan, and Liu K'o-cheng. "Peking Television University Is a Strong Fortress of the 'Three-Family Village' Gangster Inn." Jen-min jih-pao [People's Daily], June 11, 1966. Translated in Survey of China Mainland Press, No. 3723 (June 22, 1966), 1-6.

Three students of Peking Television University attack Wu Han, the president of the university, and his staff for misleading students with regard to the nature of the Great Proletarian Cultural Revolution.

Chiao-hsüeh p'i-p'an [Pedagogical Critique], August 20, 1967, published by the Editorial Committee of the Peking University Cultural Revolutionary Committee.

The issue contains "contributions by Red Guard groups

178

in the Ministry of Higher Education" and at the time of publication was "the most comprehensive review of policy conflict in higher education." For a complete translation of this publication, see Chinese Sociology and Anthropology, 2 (Fall-Winter 1969-70), 124 pp. This issue contains the following articles: "Supreme Directives"; A Commentator, "Thoroughly Destroy the Reactionary and Revisionist Educational Line of Liu [Shao-ch'i] and Teng [Hsiao-p'ing]"; The "Red Rock" Fighting Company, Peking Commune, Ministry of Higher Education; The "July 1" Fighting Company, Minister of Higher Education; The "Torch" Fighting Company, New Peking University Commune, "A Record of the Great Events in the Struggle Between the Two Lines in the Field of Higher Education"; Second Class of the Fifth Year Students, Department of Language and Literature, Peking University, "Unveiling the Dark Side of the Chinese Department's Professional Program in Classical Studies"; "Welcoming the New High Tide of the Great Educational Revolution"; "Educational Reform Activities in the Universities and Colleges"; Glossary.

China News Analysis. "Army Rule: Part VI: in Schools." No. 715 (July 5, 1968), 1-7.

————. "Education, 'Bourgeois' or Proletarian?" No. 617 (June 24, 1966), 1-7.

————. "Lu Ting-yi and Chou Yang." No. 624 (August 12, 1966), 1-7.

Chugoku kenkyu geppo [China Research Monthly]. "The Status of Educational Revolution Under the Great Cultural Revolution." September 1968. Translated in Chinese Education, 1 (Winter 1968-69), 50-66.

Two separate groups from Japan visited China during August 1968. One was a student-exchange tour group with 118 members, and the other was an educational fact-finding

179

mission with 37 members. This article, in question-answer form, is a report of a discussion that was held on August 31, 1968, with six members of these two groups.

GITTINGS, John. "Rebellious Hunan: Student Power in China." Far Eastern Economic Review, 60 (June 27, 1968), 648-650.

Analyzes the documents produced by one students' organization, the "Shen-wu-lien" (abbreviation of Hunan Provincial Proletarian Revolutionary Great Alliance Committee"), and argues that they may be the real inheritors of Mao's own rebellious youth.

GRANQVIST, Hans. The Red Guard: A Report on Mao's Revolution. Translated by Erik J. Friis. New York: Frederick A. Praeger, 1967. 159 pp.

The author observes recent pronouncements and developments of the Great Proletarian Cultural Revolution and comments in detail about Chinese flexibility in carrying out domestic programs.

HUANG, I-chang, et al. "Smash Teng T'o's Conspiracy of Inciting Youths to Oppose the Party in the Cultural Revolution." Chung-kuo ch'ing-nien pao [China Youth News], May 14, 1966. Translated in Survey of China Mainland Press, No. 3709 (June 1, 1966).

Another attack against Teng T'o and Wu Han, written by nine college students in Peking.

Hung ch'i [Red Flag]. "'Combat Self-Interest, Criticize and Repudiate Revisionism,' Carry Out Well the Struggle-Criticism-Transformation in Various Schools and Units." No. 10 (October 6, 1967). Translated in Chinese Education, 1 (Summer 1968), 11-15.

Hung-wei-ping chih luan [The Violence of Red Guards]. Taipei: Institute of Mainland China Affairs, 1967. 142 pp.

180

Briefly discusses the initiation and the background of Red Guards, their organization and activities, their tendency toward violence, factions within the Red Guards, their development and influence.

Hung-wei-ping ts'an-k'ao tzu-liao [Reference Materials on the Red Guards]. Hong Kong: Chih Luen Press, 1967. 74 pp.

Includes a chronology of the activities of Red Guards from August 1966 to February 1967; list of Red Guard publications; list of Communist leaders attacked by Red Guards.

HUNT, R. C. "The Cultural Revolution: Faith in the Field." Far Eastern Economic Review, 59 (February 8, 1968), 225-227.

An English teacher describes his experience as a member, for a week, of the "Great Proletarian Cultural Revolution Team" in the field.

HUNTER, Neale. Shanghai Journal: An Eyewitness Account of the Cultural Revolution. New York: Frederick A. Praeger, 1969. 311 pp.

The author, an Australian teacher of English at the Foreign Languages Institute in Shanghai from 1965 to 1967, presents the point of view that the Great Proletarian Cultural Revolution was a successful movement to reinstitute the works of Mao Tse-tung as the major guidelines for China's future.

Jen-min jih-pao [People's Daily]. "Bringing the Role of School Revolutionary Committees into Full Play." May 8, 1969. Translated in Survey of China Mainland Press, No. 4419 (May 20, 1966), 11-12.

Describes the conflicts between the workers' propaganda team and the school's revolutionary committee.

181

————. "Shorten the Period of Schooling and Revolutionize Education." January 9, 1968. Translated in Chinese Education, 1 (Summer 1968), 63-67.

Attack on "China's Khrushchev," Lu Ting-i, and their associates for having extended the duration of schooling so as to deprive the poor people of a chance to receive proper education and for having preserved and upheld the old educational system.

————. "Universities and Middle and Primary Schools Should All Resume Classes to Make Revolution." October 25, 1967. Translated in Chinese Education, 1 (Summer 1968), 57-60.

————. "Wipe Out the Pernicious Influence Spread by Renegade Liu Shao-chi's Revisionist Line of Education." November 29, 1968. Translated in Current Background, No. 869 (January 15, 1969).

A letter from a hsien revolutionary committee suggesting that educational revolution should be carried out by revolutionary mass criticism and repudiation. This Current Background issue is a collection of letters and articles published in the Jen-min jih-pao [People's Daily] column on entrusting production brigades to run primary schools in the countryside.

Kuang-yin hung-ch'i [Canton Printers Red Flag]. "Whither China?" 5 (March 1968), 3-6. Translated in Chinese Law and Government, 3 (Winter 1970-71), 315-347.

The views of the "ultra-left" Sheng-wu-lien, as reprinted by an unsympathetic group in Canton — the Printing Workers' United Revolutionary Committee.

KUO, T'ung. "Taking a Joyous Step Forward in the Education Revolution." Chung-kuo hsin-wen [China News], February

16, 1968. Translated in Chinese Education, 1 (Summer 1968), 3-10.

LEE, Byung Chang. "Chinese Communist Education Since the Launching of the Cultural Revolution (1966-70)" (in Chinese). Unpublished M.A. thesis, Institute of East Asian Studies, National Chengchi University, 1971.

Contains four chapters: "The Relationship Between the Chinese Cultural Tradition and Peiping's Educational Philosophy," "Changes in Educational Policy in Mainland China Between 1949 and 1965," "The Impact of the Cultural Revolution on Peiping's Educational Policy," and "Educational Reform After the Cultural Revolution.

LI, Chin-wei. Hung-wei-ping shih-lü [Facts About Red Guards]. 2nd ed. Hong Kong: World Overseas Chinese Society, 1968. 462 pp.

Based mainly on the newspapers and press releases from China (PRC), Hong Kong, and Taiwan, the author describes and analyzes the birth, emergence, organization, characteristics, factions, and sources of power of the Red Guards and their activities, including a chapter on "Educational Workers Under the Yoke of the Red Guards."

————. Hung-wei-ping shu-pien [Supplement to Facts About Red Guards]. Taipei: National War College, 1970. 246 pp.

This volume is the supplement to Facts About Red Guards which covers the Red Guards movement up to 1967. This volume brings the account up to 1970 on the Red Guards' faction fights, power struggle, the Wuhan incident, and retreat of the Red Guards, including a chapter called "The Failure of Mao Tse-tung's Educational Revolution."

LING, Ken [pseud.]. The Revenge of Heaven: Journal of a

183

Young Chinese. New York: G. P. Putnam's Sons, 1972. 413 pp.

An extensive and personalized account of the activities of one group of Red Guards from Amoy during the Cultural Revolution. The material is derived from numerous interviews of Ken Ling conducted by Ivan and Miriam London, and Chinese associates in Taiwan and elsewhere.

MEHNERT, Klaus. Peking and the New Left: At Home and Abroad. Berkeley: Center for Chinese Studies, University of California, 1969. 156 pp.

A study of the new youth organization — the "Hunan Provincial Proletarian Revolution Great Alliance Committee" (abbreviated as Shen-wu-lien) — which was formed shortly after Mao Tse-tung's visit to the province in the autumn of 1967. Eight analytical chapters on this organization focus on the relationship between the "ultra-left" factions of the Red Guards and the central leadership in Peking in the years 1967-1968. Some 21 documents related to the study are included.

New China News Agency. "Universities and Middle and Primary Schools Must Resume Classes While Making Revolution." October 24, 1967. Translated in Survey of China Mainland Press, No. 4049 (October 27, 1967), 1-3.

An editorial of Jen-min jih-pao [People's Daily] urges teachers and students to form "revolutionary great alliances" and "three-way alliances" and carry out "struggle-criticism-transformation" in their own schools by resuming classes.

PAN, Stephen, and Raymond J. de. Jaegher. Peking's Red Guards: The Great Proletarian Cultural Revolution. New York: Twin Circle Publishing Co., 1968. 462 pp.

Intended to be a service to the general public interested in knowing more about Communist China and the

184

Proletarian Cultural Revolution, the Red Guards, and their
significance in China and effect on the other parts of the
world" (Foreword).

PEARSON, Kent. "The Cultural Revolution as a New Zealand
Student Sees It." Eastern Horizon, 6 (May 1967), 32-37.

Peking Review. "On the Re-Education of Intellectuals." 38
(September 20, 1968), 16-17.

————. "Workers' Mao Tse-tung's Thought Propaganda Teams
Lead Proletarian Revolution in Education." 50
(December 13, 1968), 19-22.

SHIH, Yen-hung. "Down with the Fountainhead of Revisionist
Education." Jen-min jih-pao [People's Daily], July 18,
1967. Translated in Chinese Education, 1 (Summer
1968), 16-31.

Attacks Liu Shao-ch'i, Lu Ting-yi, and Chiang Nan-hsiang
for their "two educational systems."

Union Research Service. "Recent Developments in Educational
Revolution." 49 (November 7, 1967), 146-159.

A collection of broadcasts from provincial radio reports
on the preliminary responses to the tentative proposals
from these provinces regarding the "three-in-one" combination, putting proletarian politics to the fore, and the
method of selecting students.

————. "Reports on Educational Reform and Criticism
Against Liu Shao-ch'i's 'Dual Educational System.'"
50 (March 8, 1968), 241-255.

A number of materials translated in this issue are criticisms of the old educational system, but the majority are
studies, opinions, and instructions concerning the question
of educational reform.

185

WANG, Chao-t'ien. A Red Guard Tells His Own Story. Taipei:
Asian Peoples' Anti-Communist League, 1967. 69 pp.

An English translation of his Wo shih i-ko hung-wei-ping
[I Am a Red Guard].

WANG, Chao-t'ien. Wo shih i-ko hung-wei-ping [I Am a Red
Guard]. Taipei: Chung-kuo ta-lu wen-t'i yen-chiu so,
1967. 64 pp.

A firsthand account about the Red Guards written by
Wang Chao-t'ien, a Red Guard leader of the "East Wind
Rebel Corps" of the First Middle School of Manchouli,
Inner Mongolian Autonomous Region, who fled to Hong
Kong, then to Taiwan, on December 23, 1966.

WANG, Ch'ing-i, Ch'en Ken-huan, Wang Ch'i-hsiang, and Yuan
Kuang-ch'ing. "The Working Class Must Always Lead
Schools." Hung-ch'i [Red Flag], No. 4 (October 14, 1968).
Translated in Selections from China Mainland Magazines,
No. 634 (November 12, 1968), 14-15.

WANG, Hsueh-wen. "An Analytical Study of the Chinese Communist 'Educational Revolution.'" Issues & Studies, 4
(April 1968), 24-36.

Discusses and analyzes the development and the trends of
the educational revolution during 1966-1967.

————. Chung-kung wen-hua ta-ke-ming yü hung-wei-ping.
[Chinese Communist Great Cultural Revolution and the
Red Guards]. Taipei: Institute of International Relations,
1969. 734 pp.

This book presents an account of the Red Guards movement during the Great Proletarian Cultural Revolution.
The author devotes a chapter on each of the main topics,
such as the organization of the Red Guards, their nature
and form; functions of the factions; the Red Guards' policy

186

of "break and foster" and the mutual impact between the
Red Guards and society; the big-character wall posters;
the great alliance and great unity; export of Red Guards;
the Red Guards and education; internal conflicts and armed
struggle of the Red Guards; appraisal of the Red Guards, etc.

————. "On Mao Tse-tung's 'Educational Revolution.'" Chinese Communist Affairs, 5 (December 1968), 25-34.

WANG, Pu-shan. "Mao-kung 'kung-hsüan tui' i-nien" [One
Year of Maoist "Worker-Propaganda Team"] Fei-ch'ing
yüeh-pao [Studies on Chinese Communist Affairs], 12
(September 30, 1969), 26-31, 35.

Discusses the policy of "working class leadership" and
reviews the Workers' Mao-Tse-tung Thought Propaganda
Teams established since July 1968 on (1) the leadership
of the workers' propaganda teams stationed in schools;
(2) their functions and responsibilities; (3) the problems
they have encountered.

WU, Ping-lin. "The Socialist Philosophy of Education and the
Cultural Revolution in Communist China." Catholic Education Review, 66 (January 1968), 15-26.

The author looks at the Great Proletarian Cultural Revolution through the socialist education philosophy and points
out that the GPCR has been a process of reeducating the
Chinese people under the guidance of the socialist philosophy established by the Chinese government.

See also:

BASTID, Marianne. "Economic Necessity and Political Ideals
in Educational Reform During the Cultural Revolution."
The China Quarterly, No. 42 (April-June 1970), 16-45. [IV]

187

BRIDGHAM, Phillip. "Mao's 'Culture Revolution': Origin and
Development." The China Quarterly, No. 29 (January-
March 1967), 1-35. [III]

CCP Documents of the Great Proletarian Cultural Revolution,
1966-1967. Hong Kong: Union Research Institute, 1968.
692 pp. [I]

Centre d'Etude du Sud-Est Asiatique et de l'Extreme Orient.
"Education in Communist China." 2 vols. Brussels, Belgium, February 18-19, 1969. (Mimeographed) 245 pp. [IV]

CHI, Wen-shun. "The Great Proletarian Cultural Revolution
in Ideological Perspective." Asian Survey, 9 (August
1969), 563-579. [XII]

Chiao-yü ke-ming [Educational Revolution]. "Chronology
of the Two-Road Struggle on the Educational Front in the
Past Seventeen Years." May 6, 1967. Translated in
Chinese Education, 1 (Spring 1968), 3-58. [IV]

China Topics. "China's Education Problems." YB 427
(May 23, 1967). [I]

CHU, Hung-ti. "Education in Mainland China." Current
History, 59 (September 1970), 165-169. [IV]

Communist China, 1966. 2 vols. Hong Kong: Union Research
Institute, 1968. 251 + 282 pp. [I]

Communist China, 1967. 2 vols. Hong Kong: Union Research
Institute, 1969. 329 + 266 pp. [I]

Communist China, 1968. Hong Kong: Union Research Institute,
1969. 499 pp. [I]

Current Background. "Collection of Documents Concerning

188

the Great Proletarian Cultural Revolution." No. 852
(May 6, 1968), 1-136. [I]

—————. "The Press Campaign Against Wu Han." No. 783
(March 21, 1966), 1-63. [I]

—————. "Revolution in Education." No. 846 (February 8,
1968), 1-56. [I]

—————. "Teng T'o, His 'Evening Talks at Yenshan' and the
'Three-Family Village' Group." No. 792 (June 29, 1966),
1-73. [I]

—————. "The Wicked History of Big Conspirator, Big Ambitionist, Big Warlord P'eng Te-huai." No. 851
(April 16, 1968). 31 pp. [III]

DAI, Shen-yu. "Peking's 'Cultural Revolution.'" Current
History, 51 (September 1966), 134-139. [III]

DUTT, Gargi, and V. P. Dutt. China's Cultural Revolution.
New York: Asia Publishing House, 1970. 260 pp. [III]

ELEGANT, Robert S. Mao's Great Revolution. New York:
World Publishing Co., 1971. 478 pp. [III]

FAN, K. H., ed. The Chinese Cultural Revolution: Selected
Documents. New York: Grove Press, 1968. 320 pp. [I]

Foreign Broadcast Information Service. Communist China:
Material on Cultural Revolution. 4 vols. Washington, D.C.:
Foreign Broadcast Information Service, May 24, June 5,
June 12, June 20, 1967. 60 + 79 + 90 + 74 pp. [III]

FRASER, Stewart E. "China's International, Cultural, and
Educational Relations: With Selected Bibliography." Comparative Education Review, 13 (February 1969), 60-87. [XI]

189

FRASER, Stewart E., ed. Education and Communism in China: An Anthology of Commentary and Documents. London: Pall Mall Press, 1971. 614 pp. [I]

————. "Shattered Sino-Soviet Educational Relations." Phi Delta Kappan, 48 (February 1967), 288-293. [XI]

FRIEDMAN, Edward. "Cultural Limits of the Cultural Revolution." Asian Survey, 9 (March 1969), 188-201. [III]

GOLDMAN, Merle. "The Aftermath of China's Cultural Revolution." Current History, 61 (September 1971), 165-170. [III]

GRAY, Jack, and Patrick Cavendish. Chinese Communism in Crisis: Maoism and the Cultural Revolution. New York: Frederick A. Praeger, 1968. 279 pp. [III]

The Great Cultural Revolution in China. Compiled and edited by the Asia Research Center. Melbourne & Sydney: Paul Flesch and Co., 1968. 507 pp. [III]

The Great Power Struggle in China. Hong Kong: Asia Research Center, 1969. 503 pp. [III]

The Great Socialist Cultural Revolution in China. 10 vols. Peking: Foreign Languages Press, 1966-67. [III]

Great Victory for Chairman Mao's Revolutionary Line. Peking: Foreign Languages Press, 1967. 88 pp. [III]

GUPTA, Krishna P. "Tsinghua Experience and Higher Education in China." China Report, 7 (January-February 1971), 2-14. [VIII]

HAWKINS, John N. Educational Theory in the People's Republic of China: The Report of Ch'ien Chün-jui. Honolulu:

190

University of Hawaii Press, 1971. 120 pp. [IV]

HO, Ping-ti, and Tang Tsou, eds. China in Crisis. 2 vols. in 3.
With a Forward by Charles U. Daly. University of Chicago
Press, 1968. 803 + 484 pp. [II]

Hsin-hua-kung pao [New South China Engineering College
Journal]. "The Black Program for Fostering Intellectual
Aristocrats — Comment on the Ten-Year (1963-1973)
Plan for Cultivation of Faculty Members for South China
Engineering College." January 13, 1968. Translated in
Survey of China Mainland Press, No. 4128 (February 29,
1968), 8-12. [VIII]

HSIUNG, V. T. Red China's Cultural Revolution. New York:
Vantage Press, 1968. 188 pp. [III]

HU, Chang-tu, ed. Aspects of Chinese Education. New York:
Teachers College, Columbia University, 1969. 95 pp. [IV]

HU, Chang-tu. "The Chinese University: Target of the Cultural
Revolution." Saturday Review, 50 (August 19, 1967),
52-54. [VIII]

————. The Education of National Minorities in Communist
China. Washington, D.C.: U.S. Government Printing
Office, 1970. 30 pp. (OE-14146) [IV]

HUA, Lo-keng. "Learn Again to Dedicate Strength to Educa-
tional Revolution." Jen-min jih-pao [People's Daily],
June 8, 1969. Translated in Survey of China Mainland
Press, No. 4438 (June 17, 1969), 1-4. [XII]

ISRAEL, John. "The Red Guards in Historical Perspective:
Continuity and Change in the Chinese Youth Movement."
The China Quarterly, No. 30 (April-June 1967), 1-32. [X]

191

Jen-min jih-pao [People's Daily]. "Big Plot Exposed by a
   Big-Character Paper Posed by Seven Comrades of Peking
   University." June 2, 1966. Translated in Survey of China
   Mainland Press, No. 3719 (June 16, 1966), 6-8. [VIII]

————. "Demolish the 'Little Treasure Pagoda' System of
   Revisionist Education." December 17, 1967. Translated
   in Survey of China Mainland Press, No. 4100 (January 16,
   1968), 1-4. [VIII]

————. "Five Major Charges Against the Old Educational
   System." December 17, 1967. Translated in Survey of
   China Mainland Press, No. 4100 (January 16, 1968),
   9-11. [X]

————. "More on How 'Socialist Universities' Should Be Run."
   June 8-August 28, 1969. Translated in Current Background,
   No. 890 (September 18, 1969), 1-38. [VIII]

————. "Nanking University Exposes K'uang Ya-ming as an
   Anti-Party, Anti-Socialist and Counter-revolutionary
   Element." June 16, 1966. Translated in Survey of China
   Mainland Press, No. 3726 (June 27, 1966), 1-5. [VIII]

————. "New Peking University Marches Forward in Big
   Strides Along the Road Pointed Out by Chairman Mao."
   September 16, 1968. Translated in Survey of China Main-
   land Press, No. 4267 (September 27, 1968), 7-11. [VIII]

————. "Peking Agricultural Labor University Studies Chair-
   man Mao's Latest Instruction in a Big Way and Severely
   Repudiates China's Khrushchev's Revisionist Line for
   Education." September 6, 1968. Translated in Survey of
   China Mainland Press, No. 4260 (September 18, 1968),
   1-2. [VIII]

————. "The Red Sun Rises in the Hearts of the Red Young

192

Fighters." March 11, 1968. Translated in <u>Current Background</u>, No. 845 (May 24, 1968), 25-26. [V]

————. "Some Tentative Programs for Revolutionizing Education." November 3, 1967. Translated in <u>Current Background</u>, No. 846 (February 8, 1968), 25-28. [VIII]

————. "What Chairman Mao Says We Do." July 13, 1966. Translated in <u>Survey of China Mainland Press</u>, No. 3748 (July 28, 1966), 12-14. [VIII]

K'UNG, Fan. "Lu P'ing's Revisionist Educational Line and Its Evil Consequences." <u>Jen-min jih-pao</u> [People's Daily], July 19, 1966. Translated in <u>Survey of China Mainland Press</u>, No. 3751 (August 2, 1966), 13-20. [VIII]

<u>Kung-fei li-tz'u wen-i cheng-feng chen-hsiang</u> [The Chinese Communists' Successive Rectifications in Literary and Art Fields]. Taipei: The Sixth Division of the Kuomintang Central Committee, 1970. 365 pp. [III]

KUNG, Teh-liang. "Developments of the Chinese Communist 'Great Cultural Revolution.' " <u>Issues & Studies</u>, 3 (January 1967), 20-27. [III]

LEE, Hwa-wei. "The Recent Educational Reform in Communist China." <u>School & Society</u>, 96 (November 9, 1968), 395-400. [VIII]

LI, Ting-sheng. <u>The CCP's Persecution of Chinese Intellectuals in 1949-69</u>. Taipei: Asian People's Anti-Communist League, 1969. 67 pp. [II]

LI, Yu-sheng, et al. "Letter to CCPCC and Chairman Mao." <u>Jen-min jih-pao</u> [People's Daily], July 12, 1966. Translated in <u>Survey of China Mainland Press</u>, No. 3742 (July 20, 1966), 1-5. [VIII]

193

Long Live Victory of the Great Cultural Revolution Under the
   Dictatorship of the Proletariat. Peking: Foreign Languages
   Press, 1968. 49 pp. [I]

MA, Sitson. "We Are Slaves Who Have Been Betrayed." Life
   63 (July 14, 1967), 64-66, 69-73. [III]

MAO, Tse-tung. "Chairman Mao Tse-tung's March 7 Directive
   Concerning the Great Strategic Plan for the Great Proletarian Cultural Revolution." Jen-min jih-pao [People's
   Daily], March 8, 1968. Translated in Chinese Education,
   1 (Summer 1968), 61-62 [I]

————. "Mao Tse-tung Comments on Educational Reform."
   Issues & Studies, 6 (January 1970), 79-86. [I]

————. "Mao Tse-tung's Instructions Concerning the 'Great
   Proletarian Cultural Revolution." Translated in Current
   Background, No. 885 (July 31, 1969), 1-48. [I]

MONTAPERTO, Ronald N. "The Origins of 'Generational
   Politics': Canton, 1966." Current Scene, 7 (June 1,
   1969), 1-16. [X]

MYRDAL, Jan, and Gun Kessle. China: The Revolution Continued. Translated from the revised Swedish edition by
   Paul Britten Austin. New York: Pantheon Books, 1970.
   201 pp. [III]

NEE, Victor, and Don Layman. Cultural Revolution at Peking
   University. New York: Monthly Review Press, 1969.
   91 pp. [VIII]

New China News Agency. "Birth of Tungchi University's
   Tentative Program for Transforming Education."
   November 9, 1967. Reprinted in Survey of China Mainland
   Press, No. 4060 (November 15, 1967), 22-24. [VIII]

194

————. "Early Results of Educational Revolution at Peking Institute of Physical Culture." November 29, 1967. Translated in Survey of China Mainland Press, No. 4071 (December 1, 1967), 11-12. [VIII]

————. "East China Teachers' University on Revolution in Education." November 28, 1967. Reprinted in Survey of China Mainland Press, No. 4070 (November 30, 1967), 13-15. [VIII]

————. "How Peking Teachers' University Work Out Program for Revolutionizing Education." November 21, 1967. Reprinted in Survey of China Mainland Press, No. 4066 (November 24, 1967), 16-18. [VIII]

————. "Jen-min jih-pao Features Tentative Programs for Transforming Education." November 3, 1967. Reprinted in Survey of China Mainland Press, No. 4057 (November 8, 1967), 8-10. [VIII]

————. "Nanking University Teachers, Students Condemn Counter-revolutionary Criminal Acts of Kuang Ya-ming." June 16, 1966. Reprinted in Survey of China Mainland Press, No. 3722 (June 21, 1966), 16-17. [VIII]

————. "Peking University Committee of CCP to Be Reorganized." June 3, 1966. Reprinted in Survey of China Mainland Press, No. 3714 (June 8, 1966), 11-12. [VIII]

————. "Peking University Launches All-Out Criticism of 'China's Khrushchov.'" April 2, 1967. Reprinted in Survey of China Mainland Press, No. 3923 (April 20, 1967), 9-12. [VIII]

————. "Revolutionary Teachers and Students of Shanghai K'ungchiang Middle School Conduct Revolutionary Mass Criticism and Repudiation on the One Hand and Explore

Ways of Teaching Reform on the Other." October 24, 1967. Translated in Survey of China Mainland Press, No. 4057 (November 8, 1967), 11-14. [VI]

———. "Students All Over China Voice Their Support for the Smashing of the Old Educational System." July 15, 1966. Translated in Survey of China Mainland Press, No. 3742 (July 20, 1966). [VIII]

———. "To Be Proletarian Revolutionaries or Bourgeois Royalists ?" June 5, 1966. Reprinted in Survey of China Mainland Press, No. 3715 (June 9, 1966), 1-3. [VIII]

———. "With 'Struggle Against Selfishness and Criticism and Repudiation of Revisionism' as the Key, Whip Up a New High Tide of Educational Revolution." October 29, 1967. Translated in Survey of China Mainland Press, No. 4060 (November 15, 1967), 13-21. [VIII]

1967 Fei-ch'ing nien-pao [1967 Yearbook on Chinese Communism]. Taipei: Institute for the Study of Chinese Communist Problems, 1967. 1958 pp. [I]

1968 Fei-ch'ing nien-pao [1968 Yearbook on Chinese Communism]. Taipei: Institute for the Study of Chinese Communist Problems, 1968. 1102 pp. [I]

1969 Chung-kung nien-pao [1969 Yearbook on Chinese Communism]. 2 vols. Taipei: Institute for the Study of Chinese Communist Problems, 1969. 1700 pp. [I]

PENG, Shu-tse, Pierre Frank, Joseph Hansen, and George Novack. Behind China's "Great Cultural Revolution." New York: Merit Publishers, 1967. 63 pp. [III]

POWELL, Ralph L. "The Power of the Chinese Military." Current History, 59 (September 1970), 129-133. [III]

196

PRICE, R. F. Education in Communist China. London:
Routledge & Kegan Paul, 1970. 308 pp. [IV]

PUSEY, James R. Wu Han: Attacking the Present Through the
Past. Cambridge, Mass.: East Asian Research Center,
Harvard University, 1969. 84 pp. [III]

REECE, Bob. "Education in China: More of the Same." Far
Eastern Economic Review, 60 (June 13, 1968), 563-565. [VI]

————. "Students in China: China Revisited." Far Eastern
Economic Review, 59 (March 7, 1968), 413-418. [X]

ROBINSON, Joan. The Cultural Revolution in China. Baltimore,
Maryland: Penguin Books, 1969. 151 pp. [III]

ROBINSON, Thomas W., Richard Baum, William F. Dorrill,
Melvin Gurtov, and Harry Harding, Jr. The Cultural
Revolution in China. Berkeley: University of California
Press, 1971. 600 pp. [III]

SARGENT, Margie, Vivienne B. Shue, Thomas J. Mathews, and
Deborah S. Davis. The Cultural Revolution in the Provinces.
Cambridge, Mass.: Harvard University Press, 1971.

SCHELOCHOWZEW, S. Mao-kung wen-hua ta-ke-ming mu-chi
chi [Eyewitness Account of the Chinese Cultural Revolu-
tion]. A Chinese translation of Chinesisch Kulturrevolution aus der Nahe. Translated by the Translation Bureau,
Ministry of Defense, Republic of China. Taipei: Ministry
of National Defense, 1970. [III]

SCHICKEL, Joachim, ed. Mao Tse-tung: Der Grosse Strategische Plan. Dokumente zur Kulturrevolution. Berlin:
Edition Voltaire, 1969. 583 pp. [XIV]

SINGER, Martin. Educated Youth and the Cultural Revolution
in China. Ann Arbor, Michigan: Center for Chinese

197

Studies, the University of Michigan, 1971. 114 pp. [X]

Summary of the Forum on the Work in Literature and Art in the Armed Forces with Which Comrade Lin Piao Entrusted Comrade Chiang Ching. Peking: Foreign Languages Press, 1968. 48 pp. [III]

Ta-lu ch'ing-nien hsia-fang yün-tung ti yen-pien yü hou-kuo [The Transformation and Results of the Send-Down Movement of Mainland Chinese Youth]. Taipei: Institute of Mainland China Affairs, 1970. 19 pp. [X]

TING, Wang, ed. Pei-ching shih wen-hua ta-ke-ming yün-tung [The Great Cultural Revolution Movement in Peking City]. Hong Kong: Ming Pao Monthly, 1970. 688 pp. [I]

————, ed. P'eng Te-huai wen-t'i chuan-chi [Special Collection on the Case of P'eng Te-huai]. Hong Kong: Ming Pao Monthly, 1969. 510 pp. [I]

————, ed. Teng T'o hsüan-chi [Selected Works of Teng T'o]. Hong Kong: Ming Pao Monthly, 1969. 582 pp. [I]

————, ed. Tou-cheng chung-yang chi-kuan tang-ch'üan p'ai [Struggle Against the Clique in Authority in Central Organizations]. Hong Kong: Ming Pao Monthly, 1967. 717 pp. [I]

————, ed. Wu Han yü "Hai Jui pa-kuan" shih-chien [Wu Han and the Affair of "Dismissal of Hai Jui"]. Hong Kong: Ming Pao Monthly, 1969. 750 pp. [I]

TSANG, Chiu-sam. Society, Schools & Progress in China. London: Pergamon Press, 1968. 333 pp. [IV]

TS'UI, Min, Chang Wen-ch'ing, Ch'en Hsin-hsiu, and Kao Te-yuan. "Overthrow the Rule of Bourgeois 'Scholar-Tyrants.'" Jen-min jih-pao [People's Daily], June 6, 1966. Translated in Survey of China Mainland Press,

198

No. 3722 (June 21, 1966), 12-15. [VIII]

UHALLEY, Stephen, Jr. "The Cultural Revolution and the Attack on the 'Three-Family Village.' " The China Quarterly, No. 27 (July-September 1966), 149-161. [III]

Union Research Service. "The 'Cultural Revolution' in Colleges and Universities." 44 (July 5, 1966), 17-29. [VIII]

————. "Educational Reform After Resumption of Classes in Colleges." 48 (July 14, 1967), 42-56. [VIII]

————. "Educational Reform Plan of Peking No. 23 Secondary School." 50 (January 12, 1968), 44-56. [VI]

————. "Liu Shao-ch'i's Four Speeches Delivered at Peking College of Construction Engineering." 51 (April 26 & 30, 1968), 97-116. [VIII]

————. "Liu Shao-ch'i's 'Self-Criticism.' " 51 (May 3, 1968), 117-128. [III]

Who's Who in Communist China. 2 vols. Rev. ed. Hong Kong: Union Research Institute, 1969. 522 + 402 pp. [I]

YAO, Wen-yüan. The Working Class Must Exercise Leadership in Everything. Peking: Foreign Languages Press, 1968. 21 pp. Originally appeared in Hung-ch'i [Red Flag], No. 2 (1968). Also translated in Selections from China Mainland Magazines, No. 625 (September 3, 1968), 1-5. [III]

XIV. Mao Tse-tung's educational thought

BOORMAN, Howard L. "Mao Tse-tung as Historian." The China Quarterly, No. 28 (October-December 1966), 82-105.

CHEN, David Hsiao-hsin. "The Thought of Mao in the Light of Chinese Tradition and Revolutionary Development." Unpublished Ph.D. dissertation, University of Utah, 1970. 206 pp.

Examines the thought of Mao in the light of Chinese traditions and revolutionary development and investigates the roots of Mao's thinking in connection with ancient Chinese political philosophy, the authenticity of Maoism in relation to Marxism-Leninism, and China's contemporary revolutionary developments as related to previous revolutions in Chinese history.

China News Analysis. "Mao on Higher Education." No. 723 (August 30, 1968), 1-7.

————. "Maoism Reimposed: On Reviews." No. 559 (April 9, 1965), 1-7.

FANG, Chi. "Let Mao Tse-tung's Thought Take Root in Your Mind." Chung-kuo ch'ing-nien [Chinese Youth], No. 3, February 1, 1966. Translated in Selections from China Mainland Magazines, No. 518 (April 4, 1966), 26-27.

The author exhorts young people to learn from Mai Hsien-te, a hero who emerged after Lei Feng and Wang Chieh.

200

Jen-min jih-pao [People's Daily]. "Chairman Mao's 'March 7' Directive Is the Beacon Light Guiding Us Forward." March 12, 1968. Translated in Current Background, No. 854 (May 24, 1968), 27-33.

Reports how the teachers and students of a middle school in Shih-chia chuang, Hopei Province, were taught to study Mao's "March 7" Directive.

————. "Students Should 'In Addition to Their Studies, Learn Other Things.'" March 7, 1969. Translated in Survey of China Mainland Press, No. 4383 (March 25, 1969), 9-10.

Proposals to lay emphasis on the teaching and studying of socialist culture.

LIFTON, Robert Jay. Revolutionary Immortality: Mao Tsetung and the Chinese Cultural Revolution. New York: Random House, 1968. 178 pp.

MYERS, James Townsend. "The Apotheosis of Chairman Mao: Dynamics of the Hero Cult of the Chinese System, 1949-1967." Unpublished Ph.D. dissertation, George Washington University, 1969. 174 pp.

Deals with the manipulation of a certain category of political symbols — those pertaining to the person, thought, and deeds of Mao Tse-tung. The author examines the development of the hero cult of Mao as a political weapon, the mode of its symbol manipulation, and its manifestation in political structures.

PAYNE, Robert. Mao Tse-tung. New York: Weybright and Talley, 1969. 343 pp.

Biography with chronological table, bibliography, and index.

SCHICKEL, Joachim, ed. Mao Tse-tung: Der Grosse

Strategische Plan. Dokumente zur Kulturrevolution.
Berlin: Edition Voltaire, 1969. 583 pp.

This book consists of 16 documents by Mao Tse-tung from
1944 to 1968. Documents are divided into nine groups,
with a short introduction to each group. It commences
with "three constantly read articles": "In Memory of
Norman Bethune," "Serve the People," and "The Foolish
Old Man Who Removed the Mountains," and concludes
with a collection of instructions given by Mao during the
Cultural Revolution.

SCHRAM, Stuart R. "Mao Tse-tung as a Charismatic Leader."
Asian Survey, 7 (June 1967), 383-388.

SCHULMAN, Irwin J. "Mao as Prophet." Current Scene, 8
(July 7, 1970), 1-16.

Presents some ideas concerning the special place of
Mao Tse-tung in Chinese politics. "These ideas concern
the charismatic leadership and the role of myth as ways
of viewing Mao's relationship to the Chinese Communist
Party, and to the people of China."

WANG, Hai-jung. "A Conversation with Mao." Atlas, 21
(January 1971), 42-44.

In this verbatim interview, Mao expresses some of the
startling attitudes that lay behind his involvement in the
Cultural Revolution. In the guise of candid advice to his
niece, Wang Hai-jung, now a member of the Chinese delegation to the United Nations, Mao propounded a variety of
political-cum pedagogical axioms for the use specifically
of Red Guard activists.

WANG, Hsueh-wen. "The Problem of the Schooling System in
the Maoist Educational Reform." Issues & Studies, 6
(March, 1970), 42-55.

202

The author analyzes Mao Tse-tung's concept of educational reform and then discusses the reform of institutes of higher learning, reform of rural schools, reform of urban schools, and trends of educational revolution.

See also:

BOHLEN, Charles. "Education in China: Studies in Maoism." Far Eastern Economic Review, 67 (February 19, 1970), 19-22. [IV]

GAYN, Mark. "Mao's Last Revolution." The 1968 World Book Year Book. Chicago: Field Enterprises Educational Corporation, 1968. [III]

HSUAN, Wei-tung. "Put Mao Tse-tung's Thought in Command of Kindergarten Education." Kuang-ming jih-pao [Kuang-ming Daily], March 31, 1969 . Translated in Survey of China Mainland Press, No. 4400 (April 23, 1969), 1-6. [V]

Index to Selected Works of Mao Tse-tung. Hong Kong: Union Research Institute, 1968. 180 pp. [I]

MAO, Tse-tung. "Chairman Mao on Revolution in Education." Translated in Current Background, No. 888 (August 22, 1969), 1-20. [I]

————. "Chairman Mao Tse-tung's March 7 Directive Concerning the Great Strategic Plan for the Great Proletarian Cultural Revolution." Jen-min jih-pao [People's Daily], March 8, 1968. Translated in Chinese Education, 1 (Summer 1968), 61-62. [I]

————. "Mao Tse-tung Comments on Educational Reform." Issues & Studies, 6 (January 1970), 79-86. [I]

———. "Mao Tse-tung's Instructions Concerning the 'Great Proletarian Cultural Revolution." Translated in Current Background, No. 885 (July 31, 1969), 1-48. [I]

———. Mao Tse-tung's Quotations: The Red Guard's Handbook. Introduction by Stewart E. Fraser. Nashville, Tenn.: Peabody International Center, George Peabody College for Teachers, 1967. 312 pp. [I]

———. On Revolution and War. Edited with an Introduction and Notes by M. Rejai. Garden City, New York: Doubleday, 1969. 355 pp. [I]

———. The Political Thought of Mao Tse-tung. Selected and edited by Stuart R. Schram. Enl. & rev. ed. Harmondsworth, England: Penguin, 1969. 479 pp. [I]

———. Serve the People. In Memory of Norman Bethune. The Foolish Old Man Who Removed the Mountains. Peking: Foreign Languages Press, 1967. 11 pp. [I]

MYERS, James T. "The Fall of Chairman Mao." Current Scene, 6 (June 15, 1968), 1-18. [II]

New China News Agency. "An Example of Primary School Students in Studying the Thought of Mao Tse-tung." May 31, 1966. Translated in Survey of China Mainland Press, No. 3713 (June 7, 1966), 11-14. [V]

Problems of Communism. "More on Maoism." 16 (March-April 1967), 91-99. [III]

———. "What Is Maoism? A Symposium." 15 (September-October 1966), 1-30. [III]

SOLOMON, Richard H. "The Chinese Revolution and the Politics of Decency." Unpublished Ph.D. dissertation,

204

Massachusetts Institute of Technology, 1967. 464 pp. [IV]

Summary of the Forum on the Work in Literature and Art in
the Armed Forces with Which Comrade Lin Piao Entrusted
Comrade Chiang Ching. Peking: Foreign Languages
Press, 1968. 48 pp. [III]

WANG, Hsueh-wen. "Ten Contradictions in the Maoist Educational Revolution." Issues & Studies, 8 (October 1971),
45-60. [XII]